ALSO BY PACO UNDERHILL

Why We Buy
Call of the Mall
What Women Want

How We Eat

THE BRAVE NEW WORLD
OF FOOD AND DRINK

PACO UNDERHILL

SIMON & SCHUSTER
New York London Toronto Sydney New Delhi

Simon & Schuster
1230 Avenue of the Americas
New York, NY 10020

First Simon & Schuster hardcover edition January 2022

SIMON & SCHUSTER and colophon are registered trademarks of Simon & Schuster, Inc.

For information about special discounts for bulk purchases, please contact Simon & Schuster Special Sales at 1-866-506-1949 or business@simonandschuster.com.

The Simon & Schuster Speakers Bureau can bring authors to your live event. For more information or to book an event, contact the Simon & Schuster Speakers Bureau at 1-866-248-3049 or visit our website at www.simonspeakers.com.

Interior design by Carly Loman

Manufactured in the United States of America

10 9 8 7 6 5 4 3 2 1

Library of Congress Cataloging-in-Publication Data is available on file.

ISBN 978-1-9821-2709-1
ISBN 978-1-9821-2712-1 (ebook)

This book is dedicated to my wife, Asiye Kay Underhill

CONTENTS

Introduction: My Life in Food   *ix*

INTRODUCTION

My Life in Food

What can *I* tell you about food? I'm not a biologist or a nutritionist. Not a cookbook author or a chef. I've never stocked a supermarket shelf or raised a chicken or sold a sandwich. But I have spent countless hours over more than three decades watching people shop for food and drink. I've devoted more of my time and labor to this activity than just about anything else, including sleeping (and eating). Sounds weird, I know, but we all make our way through life doing something. If you had suggested in my youth that I'd wind up regarded as an expert in how to sell apples, or the dynamics of fast-food drive-through lines, or the geography of supermarket shelving, I'd have asked you what you were smoking. Life takes you places. I've loved every nerdy minute of mine.

This odd occupation grew out of my time as a graduate student in urban studies, learning from the legendary urbanist and author William "Holly" Whyte. To study how people move through city streets, we would stand on New York rooftops, watching the unsuspecting pedestrians below, seeing where they would slow, or stop, or hurry along, and trying to understand why. I took the methods I learned from Holly and brought them into stores, malls, restaurants—any place humans go to buy things. In time, Envirosell, the company I started in 1986, earned a long roster of clients big and small (though mostly big—research is expensive) that hired us to study their places of business and see what they were doing right or wrong or not at all.

During the past thirty-five years, my colleagues and I have worked in forty-seven countries, for more than a third of the Fortune 100 list. We've spent time in every major supermarket chain, and almost every convenience store outlet too. We've done studies for all the big grocers throughout Mexico, Canada, Latin America, China, South Africa, Southeast Asia, Europe. We've passed hours and days in convenience stores in Japan and Taiwan, mom-and-pop *tiendas* in Central America, OXXOs in Mexico, *kiranas* in India, gas stations in Scandinavia (where the Nordic world goes to buy milk), Pick n Pays in South Africa, Wongs in Peru, Extras in Brazil, METROs in Turkey, GS in Italy, Carrefour in France, Migros in Switzerland, Centras in Ireland, Tesco and Waitrose in the United Kingdom, Longo's and Loblaws in Canada, as well as airport snack-food shops all over the planet. Lots of those.

In the early years of commercial research, there were two main tools to help merchants understand how they were doing. The first was simply asking customers questions about their shopping habits and in-store behaviors. But one thing researchers learn quickly is that what people say they do and what they actually do are often very different. It's not so much that we lie—we just don't always tell the whole truth. This is a constant across all consumer research: For example, we tend to underreport how many times a day we snack, while we exaggerate the hours we spend exercising. It's human nature.

The other measuring tool was simply counting up what a store sold. It's a good way of cataloging victories, but it has its limitations. All you find out is what happened, but not why or how. And you learn nothing about what *didn't* happen, which can be just as important.

There was little attention paid to individual people in the aisles of a store—the details of precisely how they move and behave. In the mid-eighties, we came up with a system that we've used all over the world and which we still use, a method of research we call tracking. It just means that we hang around in stores and surreptitiously follow shoppers as they go about their business. Using a map of the store and a shorthand system of notation, we chart every single thing that a shopper does, from the moment they enter until they exit. For example, in a supermarket the track might report this: "A fortyish man in a tan overcoat enters at 10:32 a.m., grabs a shopping basket, walks to the right, goes to the banana display, selects a bunch, then goes to the blueberry table, picks up a package, looks at the price, puts it down, then moves to the garlic. . . ." Or we'll be hired to study just one section of the store, to see how young women shop for beer, or whether consumers look at calories or price before they choose soft drinks.

We've gotten very good at remaining unseen by shoppers, even with our clipboards and pencils (old-school) or electronic devices in hand. You learn to stand just far enough behind and to the side of someone to see what they're doing without being seen. We go undetected around 97 percent of the time, we've determined. We always say that we know we're good at this when we catch shoplifters in the act—because if they don't spot us, nobody will. When we do get busted, it's often by children, who tend to be hyperaware of their surroundings in public places.

There have been only thirty-five or forty people I rely on to perform this odd, fascinating work. Some have been with me for twenty years or more. Quite a few are theater people—actors love watching how humans behave. Our most experienced tracker, with some four hundred missions under his belt, is a former kindergarten teacher, a gentle, highly observant man who in a previous life played lead guitar in an indie band called Codeine. (Anybody remember them?)

We also use cameras and video—including time-lapse photography—to record what goes on in retail environments. We even have high-tech eyeglasses that place our cameras inside shoppers' heads (more about this later—it's pretty cool). There's a room in our head-quarters packed floor to ceiling with every form of electronic data storage ever invented, the most complete visual record of human shopping behavior ever compiled. We talk to shoppers, too, of course—usually *after* we've observed them in action, to find out what they were think-ing as they shopped. For years, we paid people leaving supermarkets to give us their shopping lists. We wanted to understand the relationship between what they meant to buy and what they bought. It was amusing how surprised people were by our weird request, and how willing they were to cooperate. It was part research, part conceptual art project.

As a result of my work, I feel free to talk to any shopper I see any-where, and to ask friendly questions (within the bounds of decency) that pop into my curious head. Whenever I see someone buying a vegetable I'm unfamiliar with, I'll ask what it is, how they prepare it, and how it tastes. Most people are happy to share their knowledge. I grant myself the same license that journalists, small children, and the elderly have to ask anybody about anything. We've learned lots of things along the way, some of which are fascinating to us but not particularly useful to clients. Women wearing light colors will almost never order red wine in a bar, we've discovered, for obvious reasons. The link between apparel and beverage choice took all us male re-searchers by surprise, but the women on the team understood at once. People who eat fast food in the restaurant's parking lot tend to drive more expensive cars than the people who eat inside. You can lower the dropout rate of a cinema concession-stand line by putting up a clock—no more anxious guessing about "How much time do I have before the movie starts?" For some reason, people don't trust their phones *or* their watches.

My fascination with food shopping was born in a U.S. Army PX—the Post Exchange, where military personnel go to shop—in Nuremberg, Germany. In the summer of 1960, I was eight years old and living in Poland thanks to my father, a diplomat stationed at the U.S. embassy in Warsaw. My experience of American life came to me mainly through Sears and Montgomery Ward catalogs. I pored through them, page by page, curious about how people back home lived. Warsaw in 1960 was behind the Iron Curtain. A huge part of the city had been leveled during World War II, and the ruins were still all around us. At that point in my life I had never been in an American store or on a shopping trip.

That summer, my father was asked to join the U.S. delegation in Montreux, Switzerland, for a conference on the Arab-Israeli conflict. We packed our 1956 Chevy station wagon with camping equipment and set out from Warsaw. Back then, there were no roadside motels or hotels in Eastern Europe, so we camped in fields until we reached the Czech-German border. Crossing the Iron Curtain was a memorable experience—the three layers of barbed wire, the plowed fields, the armed guards on the eastern side. Was I scared? Probably not. But I remember the relief on my parents' faces as we crossed the border, and the first sign I saw in western Germany: not "Welcome to Freedom" but "Drink Coca-Cola."

In Nuremberg we visited the U.S. Army PX. It was as if those Sears catalogs suddenly came to life. I walked every aisle of the store in a mild state of shock. Clothing, hardware, appliances, food, beverages— as I was growing up in what was then still a third-world setting, the idea that you could actually have all these things just for the asking blew my mind. I'd never seen so many foods in cans—soup, corn, fruit salad, beans, cherries. A whole section of frozen food! (Our summer in Switzerland was memorable for another reason. One day I was waiting for the bus that would take me to day camp when a car stopped and two very nice men inside called me by my name and asked if I wanted to go play foosball and have something to eat. Sure, I said—I had lived an extremely sheltered life—and off we went. They fed me hamburgers and French fries at a place on Lake Geneva, played foosball with me as promised, and asked lots of questions about our family, my father in particular. I answered as best I could, happy to be the center of so much friendly attention. Later that afternoon they drove me back to the bus stop just as the other kids were coming home from camp. That night I told my parents all about my marvelous day; I can still remember the look of horror on their faces. As I later learned, the Polish secret service was very curious about why a diplomat who historically worked in the Political Section of the embassy was assigned to be the American consul in Warsaw. I guess I was as good a source of information as any. Years later, at a dinner party, I met a retired CIA agent who had been stationed in Germany at the time. When he heard my name, he said he remembered investigating the incident.)

After Warsaw, my father was assigned to Kuala Lumpur, Malaysia. You can imagine the transition, going from a Soviet satellite to a former British colony on the other side of the world, from a chilly, gray, and dreary apartment to a grand Tudor-style home surrounded by tropical gardens. Ours was the only car in Malaysia with a ski rack. The food was different too. We had a houseful of staff; formal meals simply appeared on the table. I had no idea where any of it came from. I wasn't welcome in the kitchen.

At age fourteen I was shipped off to boarding school when my parents relocated to my father's next posting, in the Philippines. My food life became centered solely on what could be had in the dining room of the Milton Academy in Massachusetts. After I graduated, I got a summer job at a publishing house, and my friend Holland and I rented an apartment in Boston. My salary at Beacon Press was $70 a week. My food budget was whatever was left after rent. I was six feet four and weighed 165 pounds.

In college, I lived in a town house with five of my buddies. I remember studying the *Whole Earth Catalog*, that famous compendium of hippie living, and learning how to make yogurt out of powdered milk. I bought a slow cooker, and every evening we would put in whatever ingredients we had bought or otherwise acquired during the day, to cook overnight as we slept. After college, I moved to New York and got a job, but I didn't have much money. My friend Rip and I found an abandoned town house on the edge of the SoHo neighborhood, back before it was trendy, with a funky bar on the first floor. We talked the owner into letting us live upstairs, a three-bedroom space that had not been inhabited for twenty years. It had no kitchen, no heat, and a primitive bathroom but cost only $100 a month. Rip improvised a heater, a shower, and a stove. We were still broke, but down the block was a cheese wholesaler who put his damaged stock out in the street on Thursday nights. There were dented cases of Boursin, bruised wheels of Swiss, and more, all free for the taking, so there we went every week with empty backpacks. There's a lot you can do with cheese, it turns out. I made fondues. I made cassaroodles. I made quiches. I still like cheese.

Everybody has a formative food life, and that was mine. It's now several decades later and I continue to love everything about food and how we acquire it. My wife is happy to let me handle the household shopping. I start out with a list, but I browse each aisle of the market, and on every trip I'll pick up something unnecessary that looks inter-esting, a typical undisciplined male grocery shopper. I'm still that child dazzled by the magic and the splendors of a U.S. Army PX. To me, food shopping isn't a chore; it's a spectator sport that's also my field of scientific inquiry. In a very real sense, it's been my life's work, and therefore—fittingly—it's what has put the food on my table.

I probably don't have to point out that we've made some big changes in our shopping habits recently, especially when it comes to food. We had already begun shifting our grocery shopping from the brick-and-mortar world to online. But once COVID struck, roughly 25 percent of all grocery buying was done via apps and websites. Ordering meals from the various online delivery outfits was already popular, particu-larly among young eaters. But it became obligatory once restaurants were off-limits. Grocers prospered, even with all the tumult. Restaura-teurs and bar owners—and especially their employees—suffered terri-bly. For a spell, our cities were alive with outdoor dining—you couldn't walk down the street without having to maneuver around sidewalk tables. It was lively and fun to witness, especially in the midst of so much fear and sadness. Then winter came.

As I write this, we are still beset by a storm of crises and conflicts, one on top of another—political, environmental, economic, racial, tribal. Food plays into each and every battle. Inequality? Just look at who eats well and who doesn't. At the terrifying outset of the pan-demic, some were deemed "essential" workers, meaning their labors were necessary to feed the rest of us. Who were those brave souls? They worked at slaughterhouses and factories, on farms and in grocers and at other jobs where email and Zoom and Skype and Slack were useless, while the rest of us sat home and ate. Want to talk about inequal-ity? Greenhouse gases, carbon footprints, soil depletion? The humane treatment of animals? The encroachment of scary new technologies on the natural world? The epidemic of diet-related diseases? Meet me at the supermarket.

And yet is there anything better than food? It is as necessary to life as air or water, except it's a lot more fun and brings us much more joy. The story of food is like a record of human yearning, of our ability to provide, to invent, to create, to transform and transcend. Food is love! At least if you're doing it right.

My reason for wanting to write this book now was simple: I think that where food is concerned, we're at an inflection point unlike anything we've ever experienced before. We're definitely in "best of times/worst of times" territory.

Technology has changed nearly everything about our lives over the recent past, and food has been no exception—from how it's grown and made to the ways we acquire it. There's been a mass migration from what we quaintly thought of as the "real" world, the one made of bricks and mortar, to the digital arena, which can hardly be called unreal by now. If you've got a phone and a credit card, you can get anything edible, from any corner of the planet, delivered to you—today by a delivery person but soon by a robot or a drone, taking all human contact out of the transaction. Like something out of science fiction, at least to a twentieth-century guy like me.

Unfortunately, technology has also turned the things we eat and drink into commercial products to be engineered, manufactured, and marketed like tires or toothpaste. There's been a degradation of our food environment for profit, resulting in that *other* global pandemic, the one we scarcely acknowledge: the high rates of obesity, type 2 diabetes, associated metabolic disorders, and all the death and disability they cause. Once it was the scarcity of food that threatened our lives; today it's the abundance.

At the same time, we're in the midst of a great age of enlightenment regarding the things we eat and drink—and tech has had a huge role in that as well. We've learned to value the wisdom of nature and the importance of close contact with our food supply, of *eating local*, as the expression goes. It remains the only way to be sure that what we're getting is wholesome and healthy not just for ourselves but for the environment. Thanks to technology, we can know everything about our food, including where it was grown, and how, and by whom. We no longer ignore the inequities and the cruelties involved in our food chain.

Watching how people shop for food has given me a unique perspective on all those changes. I've been both fascinated and horrified by what I've seen, even in my own habits. We all need to get better and smarter. Maybe something in this book will help. Here's hoping.

I've tried to look at where our eating and drinking lives are headed, but it's a tricky business, I've found. We're hurtling so quickly into the future that what lies ahead today is in our rearview mirror tomorrow. And I don't own a crystal ball. But I *do* have some very smart, observant, friendly fellow travelers, and throughout this book we'll tag along with them as they make their way through the brave new world of food and drink. Their experiences and educated guesses provide a fascinating look at where we're all headed. I'll have a few observations of my own to contribute, no doubt.

A final note before we get rolling: The various encounters I report on throughout this book took place mostly pre-COVID, and then I wrote it mostly during 2020—strange, volatile times in the world I was trying to describe, like trying to hit a moving target. Hard to know how much of life would change permanently and how much (if any) would go back to what we like to think of as normal. I tried my best to steer through all that upheaval and find lessons that would last.

ONE

Getting into Supermarkets

O kay, hang on a second here: let's see if I can find a decent spot. . . .
"Do we *have* to go to the supermarket?" I can almost hear
you whine. I feel your pain, believe me. The experience leaves a lot
to be desired. And yet, despite all the upheaval in the world of eating
and drinking, it remains the place where we get most of our food. If
we're going to learn anything useful, it's going to happen here. The
first challenge we face: parking. Less of a problem if we can shop when
the rest of the world is doing something else, which accounts for the
appeal of 11:00 p.m. grocery runs. Most of us, though, are here when
everybody else is. Like right now.

This particular lot, like most, wasn't so much planned as happened
by default. Markets are almost always located in strip shopping centers, like the one we're in, meaning there are several businesses sharing
one vast, undifferentiated asphalt jungle. The result is chaos—we're all
aiming toward different destinations; we all want to be close to our
entrance, and with a clear shot at an exit. Are you surprised that more
fender benders happen here than on highways?

These lots tend to be designed by engineers with the express purpose of fitting in the greatest number of spots possible. I remember doing one of our first jobs at Target, in the late nineties, when they finally started making bigger parking spaces, in response to the growing number of SUVs on the road. They were bigger than the minivans that came before, but not as large as the pickup trucks currently popular. I'm waiting to see how much wider the spaces can get.

Adding to the challenge are the zones being carved out for shoppers who have Bought Online and Picked up In-Store—BOPIS, as they say in the trade. This is the innovation that's supposed to revolutionize the food-shopping experience. It hasn't totally taken over yet, though it makes a great deal of sense. You order online, then book a time to pick up your groceries. Once you arrive, you park in a numbered spot, text the store, and an employee delivers your groceries right into your trunk. A nice system, but it's just one more obstacle to our search for parking. It's like a blood sport out here—we're all helplessly competitive behind the wheel, even when the prize (a space twenty feet closer to the store) is fairly meaningless.

Speaking of which, that lady just took my spot! There's another good one right next to it, except some careless so-and-so left their cart blocking it. I'm usually opposed to the death penalty, but for shopping cart abandoners I'd make an exception. . . .

Attend any big sporting event or concert and you are pretty much guaranteed to find parking lot attendants wearing reflective vests (it's probably not the safest job in the world) and holding batons or flashlights or whatever airport tarmac workers use to guide pilots to their gates. What would it cost for shopping centers to hire attendants to avert the confusion, aggression, bad decision-making, and occasional collisions we witness on a regular basis, especially during busy periods? It would be worth it.

I'm not even in the store yet and I'm already tense. . . .

Parking lots in general are an interesting issue in the world of retail. They're usually identical to this one—a wasteland that's simultaneously dull and dangerous. Once you park, you hustle as quickly as possible to the store, secure in the knowledge that there won't be anything even mildly interesting to see or do on the way.

Could this parking lot be otherwise? Hard to imagine, I know. Our expectations are so low. But this could be a much different, even happier place. When you consider how much of suburban America is given over to parking lots, it seems like a waste to ask so little of them.

But supermarket parking lots are on the brink of some big changes. Not due to any inventiveness on the part of the lots' owners, or even in response to consumer demand. It's more a function of two powerful, related forces in how we will eat from now on.

One factor is the way farming itself is being transformed. Elsewhere in this book, more than once, I'll talk about how and why this is happening. It's a global movement, inspired in part by bad news—the environmental degradation of our farmland. We'll get to that a little later, but take my word for it: the news is grim.

However, there's also good news, which brings us to the second force at work here: our realization that locally grown food is better for us and for the planet. Fresher for sure. Almost surely grown without the use of industrial-level pesticides, which at some point end up in our air and water. Delivered to us without the need for planes, ships, trains, or refrigerated tractor-trailers. Beneficial to the local economy. How many reasons do we need?

How will all that play out in this godforsaken place? Here's one way: we'll grow food here.

Instead of certain crops being farmed far away and then transported to stores, they will grow in greenhouses, which can be built pretty much anywhere. We won't even have to enter the store to shop. There will be a farmer—almost certainly someone young, probably idealistic and well educated, enthused about what they're growing and especially how, and likely in love with the cutting-edge technology that's behind this megashift in the food chain.

You'll just choose what you want—today I happen to need some spinach, lettuce, arugula, basil, and rosemary—and, a few snips of the shears later, it's yours. All grown year-round and hydroponically, meaning without soil and not dependent on rainwater. Wrapped in paper instead of plastic, probably, in keeping with the green vibe. Handed to you with a smile. Couldn't be any fresher unless you grew it in your kitchen.

I love it. You're going to love it too.

And you might not even need to build a greenhouse. Today, steel shipping containers are being repurposed—recycled—as controlled-environment farming modules. The plants will be nourished by grow lights and irrigated by sophisticated watering systems, so we're not entirely independent of electrical power. But in the right setting, solar energy could take care of those needs too.

The crops likely will be on the smaller side, like leafy greens, sprouts, herbs, peppers, cherry tomatoes, berries, stuff like that. You could grow watermelons this way, but you won't get very many out of a greenhouse.

This may sound like a scenario dreamed up by some starry-eyed Green New Deal visionary, but big corporations—Walmart!—are seriously looking at on-site growing technology. Not because it's such a cool concept, but because it has the potential to solve some major food supply crises in our near future, and also be profitable, which is the key element that will make all this a reality someday soon.

Of course, a greenhouse in this lot will make the competition for parking even worse. But there are other changes in how we buy food that will cut down on the number of people coming here anyway. This means that the store itself is going to shrink and become less super, which won't be such a bad thing. So maybe a smaller lot won't be a big problem.

Let's see—how else could we turn the supermarket trip into something more than a dreaded chore?

Food trucks? An entire food court of food trucks! Depending on what part of the country we're in, this could wind up the best, most exciting place to dine in town—it's going to be like one big internationalist motorized buffet. (Remember when we used to call them roach coaches? The worst kind of belly fill? Not today.) The beauty of food trucks wherever they show up—and they're everywhere, on a global scale—is that they're almost always owned and run by people who love the food they're serving. It's a perfect setup for entrepreneurs on a tight budget, which, in America today, is often someone recently arrived from another country, eager to share the cuisine and the culture they brought with them. Their food tends to be fresh, authentic, inexpensive, and made at home with love and pride. This will come in especially handy once you get away from cities, because suburbs and exurbs often are underserved by food-delivery outfits. And there's no reason food trucks can't deliver too.

Okay, what more can we do to instill joy into this place? The obvious thing would be to retrofit the lot with proper infrastructure, meaning electrical outlets, improved lighting (assuming there's any lighting at all, which isn't always the case), plumbing, heating, Wi-Fi. Once that happens, the sky's the limit. It would make possible some kind of permanent structure built to hold bathrooms, ATMs, charging stations, child care, a place to chill out and watch movies or college football on big-screen TVs while we wait for Mom or Dad or whoever is doing the shopping today.

How about a bandshell, an outdoor concert venue, or a pop-up theater? After dark, an open-air cinema? During COVID's strictest periods of social distancing, any such activity spaces were a blessing. Almost anything would be an improvement over this parking lot or any other.

In some countries, like Thailand and South Korea, there are special sections of parking lots reserved for women shoppers. It might come as a surprise to men that even in supermarket lots, women walking alone are not spared the unwanted attentions and remarks of crude and piggish guys. Hard to imagine, I know—are there men who leave the house to shop for groceries and decide to harass a few women too? Women also deserve their own sections here because they are more likely to be managing kids and strollers and therefore need a little extra consideration.

Before we go inside, I want to move in the opposite direction, all the way back to the farthest extremity of the lot. *Please.* I have my reasons.

I can no longer count the number of times I have done what we call walk-throughs or store clinics with supermarket and shopping center executives. These jaunts consist of me traveling around the world to places just like where we are now and telling the business-men and -women what they're doing wrong and what they could do better. It is one of the most enjoyable parts of my job. We start our sessions as far as possible from the entrance. Invariably, the execs give me funny looks, wondering what this has to do with the store they run. But here, I explain, is where your store truly begins—at the first place the shopper can glimpse it. Here is where you enter the customer's consciousness. From down the block, across the street, the edge of the parking lot.

Notice anything? Me neither. There's nothing to notice—just a bland, flat, featureless building, probably beige or gray, with a not-so-grand entrance. This structure virtually promises you a boring time. The only visual element, most likely, is the store's name and maybe a logo. Shop 'n' Drop or something catchy like that.

In the past, merchants understood. A cobbler had a sign shaped like a shoe. The barber had a red-and-white-striped pole. Did that really symbolize the days when barbers provided medical treatment by bleeding sick people? So it seems. I wouldn't trust my barber to perform surgery on me, but I still like his sign. The pawnshop has a fixture with three gold balls. A butcher might deploy a barnyard animal logo. There are plenty of smiling cows welcoming customers inside. In Europe, I've seen equine butchers with cartoony horse heads as their logos. Granted, it's a little creepy, but it gets the message across.

The supermarket? Chances are there's not even a vaguely food-like image on the exterior. Or any image at all. Ironically, the very first self-serve supermarket, the Piggly Wiggly, founded in 1916, had a grinning pig as its logo. Still does. They even sell T-shirts featuring that cute little porker. Can you imagine wearing your supermarket's T-shirt?

Okay, we've trudged through the lot and we've reached the doors. We can finally pass from out here to in there.

Hang on. Not quite yet.

There's a principle that governs any transition we make from one physical environment into another—like now, for example, as we step from outdoors to indoors, from the lot into the store. It's what we call the transition zone.

We make this voyage, from one physical area into another, countless times a day. We do it so often it barely registers. But our brains and bodies know. When you enter a house, invariably there's a space just inside the door—"vestibule" being the decorous term, which originated in ancient Roman architecture, though the Greeks employed them too. The space that connected out there to in here. Same as the lobby you find in every office building, hospital, or any other public structure.

We've spent countless hours explaining the significance of this to our clients. We try to convince them to keep this transition zone—this landing pad—clear. There's no point trying to sell somebody something here, or asking them to absorb a written message from a sign. We've shot plenty of video of people entering malls, stores, restaurants, and other spaces, and we've witnessed exactly how human beings perform in such moments. First, we slow down. Our feet tell our brains that the flooring feels different, and we make the subtle shifts necessary to handle that. Maybe there's a step up or down, or a change from asphalt or grass to linoleum, tile, or carpeting. The light is suddenly different too—brighter, or dimmer, or coming from a different direction. And so, our pupils must also adjust. The sounds and smells are different. There's a lot going on.

Did the store put a rack of flyers immediately inside the door, down at about waist level? We're not going to see it. Are the shopping baskets just two steps in, next to the flyers? We'll speed right by them. Are they on the left side of the entrance instead of the right? Now we'll never see them.

Where *are* we looking? Probably downward. That's pure self-preservation. We don't want to trip and fall or crash into anything or anybody.

I'm sure that back at some architect or designer's studio, this entryway was left more or less bare, as it should be. It probably stayed that way for, oh, a week or two. Then stuff migrated in, as stuff always seems to do, everywhere. Cardboard stands holding packages of potato chips, or cookies, or some other nonnecessities, on the theory (I guess) that even speeding shoppers won't be able to resist a snack bargain. Or looming banks of bottled water, case upon case. Is there a shopper who really hits the brakes two steps inside the store to grab a case of water?

In the early, panicky days of the lockdown, most market entrance areas were transformed into hot zones. They usually featured an employee or two acting as combination doorperson/security guard, allowing people in if they were properly masked, and sometimes gloved, and even then only when other shoppers were leaving, to allow for ample social distancing. There were hand sanitizer stations. Glove dispensers. Visual guides reminding us how long six feet actually is. Signs instructing us where and how to walk once we got inside. Arrows on the floor. You might have predicted, as I did, that these restrictions would be in place for a good long time. You probably wondered if things would ever return to "normal." Instead, we kept our masks on as required but pretty much abandoned all those other protections. Even when infections began surging back to peak levels, we didn't revert to first-wave paranoia.

For a while, though, supermarkets were swamped by shoppers in mortal fear of running out of bread, or disinfectant spray, or toilet paper, or yeast. You couldn't find frozen broccoli, or frozen pizza either. Pasta? I know people who at this moment still have a year's worth crowding their pantry shelves. Along with all that, we each began to recalibrate the size of our spatial bubble—the amount of separation from one another we require in order to feel safe. Before long, though, those bubbles began shrinking back to the old size.

Anyway, we're blocking the entrance. Let's go inside. It's time.

But wait, before we do . . .

TWO

The Citified Get Countrified (and Vice Versa)

Before we plunge into the modern supermarket, I thought we'd take a step out of time, into a place that is both the past and the future—one future, at least—of our relationship with food, where the old meets the next.

On my relentlessly urban—noisy, jam-packed, car- and truck- and bus-exhaust-perfumed—walk home from the office, on at least three days a week (four if I work Saturdays), I get to stroll through one of the glories of the city eater: the open-air farmers market. This one, at Union Square, is the flagship of New York City's Greenmarket system, and largest of the fifty or so open-air markets throughout the city.

As with most farmers markets, this one exists in a space intended for something else. The broad sidewalk in front of the park here is normally just that—a big expanse of bare concrete, a place for people to walk in a city where pedestrian space is usually crunched. Especially in this part of town, which visitors—mainly young ones—frequent. A lot. Union Square once was farmland, then a potter's field, and finally a great urban crossroads, where Broadway, 14th Street, University Place, and Fourth Avenue all converge, the boundary of four desirable residential neighborhoods (Gramercy Park, Flatiron, Chelsea, Greenwich Village). On opening day of this market, in 1976, seven farmers showed up, and by noon they sold everything they brought.

This is the future of back to nature as envisioned by New York City, meaning it's governed by a thirty-three-page document of rules and regulations that covers everything from the precise meaning of the word "local" (all food for sale must be grown and processed within a circle that extends no more than 250 miles from city limits) to the contents of the food (no GMOs, no trans fats, no weird non-food additives, no plastic packaging). Even the baked goods should be made completely from scratch and must "avoid ingredients that do not support our mission."

Ah, yes, this is a market with a mission: started amid the heady fumes of the first Earth Day back in the seventies, and constantly evolving and renewing and brimming ever since, maybe the only common ground left where the citified meets the countrified, clearly at the forefront of . . . of *what*? Of whatever forces are leading us into the heart of twenty-first-century foodways.

Not that there's anything remotely new about the idea of farmers selling their goods directly to eaters. That, of course, has been going on since, well, whenever it was that agriculture (which is at least twelve thousand years old) and trade (even older) joined forces. But the postindustrial model is definitely in vogue: According to the U.S. Department of Agriculture, in 1994 there were 1,755 marketplaces in American cities and suburbs where farmers sold directly to buyers. By 2019, there were 8,771 and growing. The USDA even has its own farmers market, in Washington, D.C., and does its best to expand the reach of small growers through programs that make it easier for people on food stamps and for schoolchildren to take advantage of these places.

12

On a summer's day, you stroll through the Union Square farmers market thinking there's absolutely nothing edible or drinkable that isn't available and in abundance. Nothing tropical, of course. No pineapples. But an awful lot during the time of the year when northeastern farmers are up to their eyeballs in crops.

But you might reasonably wonder what there could be to shop for here in the middle of winter. The answer would be: still quite a lot. Once, the farmers market was a highly seasonal enterprise—like agriculture itself. If the farmer can't grow it, she can't sell it, and so you'd expect this place to be a ghost town from autumn to spring.

But farmers are smarter than that. They must be, or they'd be ex-farmers. It's hard—increasingly harder—to make a living solely by nature's dictates.

We're seeing the evolution of the farmers market as it becomes a twelve-month proposition, as companion—and competition—to all other ways we have of buying and selling food. Thanks to modern technology, apples and some vegetables can be stored in pressurized chambers and kept fresh year-round. Technology helped big food get bigger in the twentieth century, but in the twenty-first, tech is helping us get smaller, more efficient, more democratic. And as the market concept has matured, it has become a venue not simply for farmers. Now it's home to vendors who don't sell fruits or vegetables or meat or anything else that's farmed per se, but rather things they've made from locally farmed ingredients: pies, cookies, bread, cakes, granola, of course, and spirits, wine, beer, yes, plus potato chips and pretzels. In addition to the standard pork, chicken, and beef, now there's bound to be somebody selling bison burgers, impala cutlets, or other new-age meats that make their way onto some of our tables. No matter what the weather, there's always going to be a kimchi lady. There will be the bee person, too, with honey coming from various parts of New York

13

City, where the issue isn't just sweetness but specific allergen protection based on the neighborhood where the bees live. (Urban beekeeping is amazing.) We'll also find everything you can possibly make out of milk, including milk itself but also yogurt, kefir, butter, ice cream, and a thousand different cheeses.

In many cases, the sellers have both grown the ingredients and turned them into something wonderful to eat or drink. They do that because it's a good way to maximize profits. An apple is worth more baked into a pie or dried and mixed with granola or trail mix than it is sold as nature made it, even accounting for the extra labor and ingredients.

And everything here, whether grown or crafted, is locally sourced, we know, because the vendors are by and large honorable people—but also because Greenmarket New York employs inspectors whose job it is to make sure nobody tries to bend the rules, which happens, of course. Farmers are human too.

While we marvel at the diversity of locally grown agriculture, we can also take in the spectacle of city shoppers in all their various forms. This is the other appeal of farmers markets—we get to watch other people shop, in a way that doesn't happen in the supermarket, where we're herded through aisle after aisle of tall shelves that render our fellow shoppers invisible, almost like mice moving through a maze in search of that cheese (literally). As a result, we can't satisfy our normal human curiosity to check out what everybody else is buying (and eating). At the farmers market, we're all exposed to one another's inquisitive—or nosy—gaze.

Part of what makes my own farmers market experience so fascinating is that I get to see the whole spectrum of local fauna—from movie and TV stars without their makeup on, wearing the standard jeans, puffy jackets, and wool caps, to NYU students from all corners of the globe, and every other type of New Yorker.

The amount of culinary education that goes on at open-air markets also vastly exceeds what happens either in stores or when shopping for food online. Go to a market, pick out the weirdest vegetable you can find, the one that's a complete mystery to you, and ask the farmer how to prepare it. I guarantee you'll get a quickie cooking lesson—maybe more than one, depending on how many shoppers are eavesdropping.

I like talking to the person who grew something or made something for me. I think farmers get a kick out of meeting the people who depend on them for the stuff of life. If nothing else, they're amused by us city slickers. Selling what they grow directly to the person who is going to consume it is an affirmation of the skill and effort required in farming. If a farmer sells produce to a wholesaler, there may be pride in its quality or pleasure in the monetary transaction, but the primeval joy of one person handing food to another is missing.

As great as farmers markets may be, they still leave lots of room in the food chain. We'll always have to buy our Lucky Charms and nacho-flavored Doritos somewhere. And we'll never totally give up our desire for produce when it's out of season or otherwise inaccessible—we let that genie out of the bottle long ago. Bananas are the most popular fruit in the world, but they grow only in a narrow tropical belt. We've become addicted to avocados as part of the modern health fanatic's diet, but you won't find many growing year-round above the Mexican border. And, let's face it, sometimes it's just easier to zip into the supermarket or convenience store for eggs or a couple apples or some grape jelly and sliced bread. So, no matter how much they expand, farmers markets won't fit every need or cure every ill. Nor should they. Let a hundred zucchini flowers bloom.

———

When I was a child back in the fifties, I encountered my first farmers market halfway between our apartment in Warsaw, Poland, and the American embassy, where my father worked. We went almost every week to buy a lot of what we ate.

I loved going. The ground was covered in a mixture of dirt and the discarded outer leaves of cabbages, which shoppers had tramped down into a green-brown mud. The market was run mostly by rural women with kerchiefs tied around their heads. The sounds of laughter and haggling over mountains of dirty, ripe carrots, potatoes, onions, and apples are what I remember best. The women all wore the same kind of boots, thick with only a vague distinction between right and left. One day I watched someone take a boot off and I saw that, instead of a sock, she had a long scarf wrapped around her foot and ankle for a custom fit. My mother had her favorite vendors—I never understood why, but that was part of the experience, visiting one friendly face after another. I was fascinated by the knives they used to trim the vegetables and chop away the rough parts before bagging them. The women never seemed to look at what they were doing, and yet I never saw a finger cut off—and believe me, I looked.

Later, after my father had been reassigned to Korea, we shopped the farmers markets in Seoul. Again, there was that layer of cabbage leaves ground down into the mud, evidence of the national taste for kimchi, which every family made at home. Once more, I was struck by the noisy friendliness of the transactions, mostly women selling to women. That sisterhood of garden to table is global.

Now, six decades later, I'm still buying the same way. Mary has a stand in the farmers market near my home. She reminds me of the women running the stands in Warsaw. I think the farmers market movement is partly about female empowerment—elevating the nurturing impulse to a broader scale, powerful enough to challenge the traditional bad old ways of the food system and giving women an economy they control. Mary has a ready smile and a friendly way about her. She has a Jersey accent and loves to steer me toward things she herself picked. She doesn't know my name or anything about me, but she's confident giving me food advice, and I trust her. I don't question the prices and I never count the change. When she's not there I ask after her and the other workers respond with respect and love. "Mary's home taking care of her sick mother this weekend." I hear the goddess worship in their voices.

I have a friend, Janie, who ran a small organic farm outside of Columbus, Ohio. This was after she retired as an executive in the movie business, where she was a heavy hitter. She didn't look Hollywood. She was short and strong with curly gray hair and a big, beautiful smile. She took her produce to the farmers market in Columbus every Saturday and always sold out hours before everyone else. Maybe it was her business background, but she understood visual merchandising. Each thing she sold had its own sign that stressed how special it was. Not just *tomatoes* but "Monitor Organic Heirlooms." Even if you didn't know a thing about tomatoes, you could tell that she was offering you something extraordinary. Whenever I see an underperforming stand at a farmers market, I think of Janie and what she could teach them. She brought some sophisticated theatricality to a place where you'd least expect to find it, but the truth is that all retail spaces are theatrical. The only distinction is that some are good at it and some are not. Even the most rustic-looking farm stand is the result of many choices and decisions. Do we sell the produce as it was picked, or cleaned and trimmed? In wicker baskets or battered plastic crates? The theater of the farmers market excuses some haphazard flourishes. The flaws in presentation contribute to the air of authenticity.

If you walk the streets of European and South American cities, you'll find open-air markets all over the place. Unlike here in the States, there's nothing new or novel—they've been doing it for centuries and never got out of the habit. Some markets are right on the street, others in giant sheds divided into stalls. They sell fruits, vegetables, herbs, meats and fish, olive oil, also bread, cheese, and other prepared foods. Not all the sellers are farmers, and not all the produce is hyper-local. Vendors go to the wholesale markets to get the produce they sell, just like any grocer does.

Some of the appeal to shoppers is pure convenience. In Brazil, these markets pop up close to public transportation and are designed for quick sales to people heading home from work. A paper bag of vegetables or fruit, price marked right on it—no weighing, just grab, pay, and go.

Would that work alongside our commuter train stations or bus stops, or even in New York's subway system? It might. There you can buy newspapers, candy, and soft-core porn, so why not fruits and vegetables? You'd be able to eat a healthy snack on the way home and save yourself a stop at the supermarket.

In São Paulo, they added restaurants on the balconies overlooking the central marketplace, a reinterpretation of farm-to-table. The restaurants serve the same products being sold down below. Many of the stalls are nicely designed, with vitrines and gorgeous displays—but this isn't the kind of farmers market we Americans have fallen in love with. It doesn't harken back to our agrarian roots but to a nineteenth-century urban European model.

Our farmers market movement has traditionally been run by nonprofits, with an unstated progressive/do-gooder political impulse behind the desire to bring farmers and shoppers together. That one-to-one connection between grower and eater is a fundamental shift in how we acquire the things we feed ourselves and our families. It's changing the health of our environment for the better, so even the planet benefits. The system gives small farmers a chance to make or find markets not dominated by the giants. No one is getting rich, but it's a viable and rewarding way of life. The farmer works long hours yet feels good about what she's doing. There's enough money to help his kids pay for college, and maybe take a winter vacation every few years.

I think most people who buy at these markets feel good even beyond what they purchase, for a variety of reasons. One shopper is the dedicated, environmentally aware foodie—the one who wants only what's fresh, local, in season, and grown with love and care for the earth. This person prefers to buy their fiddlehead ferns, hen-of-the-woods mushrooms, Japanese eggplant, and pastured blue-green eggs from a grower who isn't dumping hazardous agricultural chemicals into the soil or depleting its nutrients. An ethical farmer but a somewhat sophisticated one, too, who is at the forefront of culinary trends, who pays attention to what people are eating right now. This buyer is usually willing to pay more than most traditional stores would charge. Restaurant chefs fit into this category.

Another fan is here mainly for the value. They're not looking for the esoteric or even the organic—they want the regular stuff (tomatoes, corn, peppers, lettuce, onions), straight from the farm, without the middleman, meaning cheaper than the supermarket but also fresh and ripe and tasty. Often, these shoppers are recent immigrants from rural cultures, so they really know their beans.

Then there's the rest of us. We like to try new things as long as they taste good and our families will try them. We don't mind paying a little more for healthy, fresh food, but we're not connoisseurs for whom price is no object.

One drawback to most farmers markets, including this one, is also part of their charm—the ad hoc, ramshackle spirit of turning a parking lot, or a schoolyard, or the green space in front of a public building into a marketplace once or twice a week. That means there's usually no permanent infrastructure—no electricity to run refrigerators and freezers, no lighting to allow night markets, no covered structures to make shopping possible in cold and wind and rain or snow. And what happens if you need to shop on a nonmarket day? We've grown accustomed to being able to buy anything, any day, at any time. This, too, inhibits the ability of the market movement to reach even deeper into the American food environment. But if the markets became too solid, too fixed, wouldn't they lose their spirit?

———

It makes perfect sense that the question of dirt would be a salient one at the farmers market. On the one hand, some soil on the produce—particularly on root vegetables—might be a good thing. It's like a label that says: "This is as fresh as can be, straight from the fields; we didn't even stop to brush it off!" It's a way of distinguishing the goods here from the power-washed, sanitized, shrink-wrapped food at the supermarket—which, by contrast, is suspiciously clean.

On the other hand, who wants dirty food?

The question of cleanliness comes up in every category of retailing. A run-down fitting room, a shabby bathroom, dusty shelves, smeared mirrors or windows—they have nothing to do with what we're buying, exactly, but they are all major turnoffs. Nowhere is cleanliness more important than when we're buying food, whether at a shop or farmers market or restaurant. And in our post-pandemic world, our radar for clean will have been heightened.

Over the decades, we've noticed something maybe not so surprising about dirt—women are much more sensitive to it than men are. When we talk to women about a particular store, they will often bring up cleanliness (or its lack) without being asked. Men almost never do.

We worked with a Mexican supermarket chain where all the cleaning was done after store hours, which, from a practical point of view, makes perfect sense. It's how most stores do it. Nobody wants to smell disinfectant when they're shopping for fresh-baked bread or strawberries. But a woman executive of the company said she thought employees should be cleaning the stores continually, as the need arose, and so they tried it. Floors were swept and mopped, glass doors were wiped, and so on, all day.

When the managers read the customer comment cards, they discovered that women shoppers noticed—and appreciated—the cleaning activity. Labor costs were unchanged, but the perception of cleanliness rose. (The Mexican supermarket industry is one of the most progressive and exciting in the world—and one reason is the presence of women in management.)

Men shoppers either didn't see the difference or didn't care. I don't think it's because men are that much filthier than women. I think we just don't perceive dirt the way women do. I believe this also accounts for the fact that even in the most egalitarian households, women often complain that men don't do their share of the cleaning. Women's standards are just higher when it comes to dirt (among other things).

Today, at the farmers market, the same phenomenon is evident. There's a guy selling garlic that is caked with dried soil. His cardboard containers aren't so appetizing either. Two stands away, organic cherry tomatoes are as clean and shiny as buttons, in perfect, spotless little baskets. I won't bother to tell you the gender of that stand's boss.

A little farther on, there's a vendor with a variety of herbed cheeses, all of which look delicious, encased in shrink-wrap and displayed in plastic racks—all which could use a good cleaning. The cheese is fully protected, so does it really matter what the racks look like? It will to many buyers, I guarantee. Remember that most shoppers here (and everywhere) are women.

Next to the cheese guy is a stand selling chicken—halves and parts. The poultry is bagged in clear plastic and on ice, displayed in racks similar to the ones next door. Except these are immaculate.

"I've been noticing that your stand is cleaner than most of what I see here," I tell the woman running the stand.

"Right!"

"If you look at the difference, the guys at the stand over there haven't wiped those racks down in a while, but you have, correct?"

She just nods.

"My theory," I say, "is that a stand run by women tends to have a better, uh . . ."

"It's cleaner!" She laughs.

"You think that's true too?" I ask.

"Yes, I have to agree with you."

"Do you think women have higher standards?"

"Yes! I—The guys that help us? If an egg breaks, they just throw it away and wipe off the table. But they don't wash it with water or spray it."

"Uh-huh."

"We *wash* it. You know what I mean? We look at it and say, 'Ew, this is *gross!*'"

Speaking of dirty food, I had a little epiphany this week at my local organic-food store. They sell the same radishes that I get at the farmers market, except in the store they're completely clean, because somewhere along the way, somebody's job was to wash them and make them presentable. Now, there's the aesthetic difference, which I've already discussed. I may be a germophobe who would never buy anything with visible dirt, even if it's the clean dirt of the farm.

But there's also another consideration: every time food is touched by a person in the supply chain, its cost goes up. Even the lowest-wage radish cleaner must be paid. Throughout the system that brings our food to us, wherever it originates, every time anything is touched by a human being, its environmental impact also increases. An apple that's grown forty miles away is touched by the picker, the cleaner, the packer, and the unpacker who just sold it to you. Compare that to a mango, which was grown and harvested in the tropics, thousands of miles away, and then transported in a shipping container that had to be loaded and unloaded, and then has likely gone through a wholesaler's warehouse, to an inspector or two, and then to the loader, the trucker, the grocer . . . a lot of hands. Each step adds to the cost, environmental and otherwise.

Still, from my personal perspective, I have to ask: Do I feel like washing and trimming radishes before I can eat them? Do I really need one more kitchen job to do before I can sit down to dinner?

Right now, I confess, I have some very clean radishes in my bag on the way home.

Onward.

Now, maybe not everybody needs purple potato chips. Maybe *nobody* needs purple potato chips. But I believe this is a richer, finer world with purple potato chips in it. I just found some here thanks to a small farmer from Long Island who has brought in, along with lots of potatoes, five different kinds of chips, each made from a different variety of tuber. Including purple ones. And you know what? They taste good. They taste . . . *purple*.

Another thing—the farmer has set out bowls with the different varieties of chips they make, so you can sample before you buy. This is something you see a lot here and is a bedrock principle of smart retailing: if you let people try something, they are much more likely to buy it, whether it's skin lotion, beef jerky, or potato chips. Here's one reason why big corporate food is so boring. If they were truly interested in innovation, they'd find more compelling ways to introduce us to new products. Like giving us samples, right there in the supermarket aisle. But those massive corporations, which employ armies of extremely smart people with fancy degrees, either don't know how to offer you samples or don't believe it's worth the effort. Look around the modern supermarket and see the same sad truth: thousands of things meant to be eaten or drunk, and yet no way to try them without paying for them first.

Dumb.

This farmers market is ringed with supermarkets, like the Whole Foods just to the south—you can stand in the store and look down on the market from one of the big windows. Back when the market opened, store owners bitched—understandably—at the thought of the city fostering a new form of food retailing, which would no doubt undercut the brick-and-mortar stores. Somehow, everybody thrives.

For all the advantages and conveniences of modern major retail, it can't engender the same emotions a small farmer can—trust being among the most important. For if there's one thing that has changed over the past forty or fifty years in our relationship with big food corporations, it's our loss of trust. Here, at the market, I'm buying squash from a guy whose fingernails are still dirty from unloading it. This kimchi was made in her own kitchen by the woman who's telling me how she serves it. These Amish families raised, slaughtered, and cleaned the chickens they're selling. Now, compare them to the people working at your local supermarket, who are getting paid by the hour to do their not particularly great job and who—understandably—can't wait to go home and put their feet up. There's just a different level of commitment to the food you're going to take home and eat and feed to the people you love.

The farmers market brings an air of wholesomeness and freshness to everything sold there. You trust the food hasn't gone through a middleman or sat around on a truck or in a warehouse for weeks. The irony is that much of the produce sold at any supermarket is local too. Not out of any ethical motivation—local produce is cheaper because of lower transportation costs. And stores love announcing that the apples, or corn, are local. Supermarkets are in the business of making customers happy.

Here's a stand selling bread and other baked goods. There are a lot of vendors selling bread here today. It could be the market's biggest category—bread and baked goods. It's really noticeable when it's too cold out for most fresh produce vendors. It's not news that we Americans love grain-based foods and desserts—probably too much. Desserts and foods made with wheat flour (including pizza) are the number-one source of calories in the American diet. At the same time, we all sense that the mass-produced versions are not very healthy—they're not only high calorie but full of additives and preservatives and who knows what. We reject unhealthy corporate bread by buying baked goods here, made by small producers who at least give the appearance of being health conscious, meaning conscious of *our* health.

Again, it comes back to one of the main appeals of the farmers market: we assume that these bakers eat their own goods, so they make them with the best ingredients and the fewest industrial processes, and in ways that do the smallest damage possible to the soil and the environment. Is that assumption always correct? You'd have to be a scientist to know for sure. But it sure seems that way, and that's good enough for most of us.

Onward, to the vendor next door.

"Would you like to taste?"

"It's a little early in the day for me."

We're at the artisanal vodka stand. Made from local potatoes.

"Oh, it is *not* too early."

"It's *not?*"

"Here, the cups are tiny."

"Okay. Tell me, what is the ratio between trial and purchase here? If you hand out samples to four people, will one of them buy? Or is this just an evangelical act?"

"Well, I'm not keeping any statistics here."

"Okay."

"But I have to tell you, a lot of people think this is an open bar, and like—we're just like giving away vodka."

"Right."

"It's really pricey and it's very hard to make. This bottle alone is twenty-eight dollars. And we just break even with that, you know? It's real potato sipping vodka. It's a really high-end product."

"Okay, I get it."

"I mean, it's really *good*. And what do you think about it?"

"Well," I say, "given that I've spent thirty-five years working for the adult-beverage industry—"

"Yeah . . . ?"

"All of them are shitting in their pants because of people like you."

"Well, you know, okay, that a lot of their stuff is crap, and they're not farmers. They don't grow their own product."

Onward.

The young woman behind the counter nods toward a whole array of the various kinds of kimchi she makes.

"And what is the ratio of sampling to purchase? If you hand out ten samples, how many people end up buying?"

"I would say almost eight of them buy."

"Eight!"

"Yeah."

"Wow. So—"

"They would taste it, they would say it's good, they will buy it."

She sells to 80 percent of people who try! Hard to believe every food store isn't a sampling extravaganza.

Onward.

Does anybody really go to a farmers market to buy $70 bottles of whiskey? Good question.

"Hey, how are you?"

"Good, good."

"How often do you sell one of those?"

"That big bottle, not so often. I only bring two or three of those here."

"Okay, so why . . ."

"I sell more small bottles."

"Okay, but how often does somebody come and buy a big bottle from you?"

"Often enough."

"Oh yeah?"

"Yeah."

"That's very cool, that somebody can walk through a farmers market and be able to drop seventy dollars on a bottle of whiskey."

"There's— He's not here today, he sells a bottle that costs almost one hundred dollars."

"Really?"

"It's not about the money," he says. "It's more the quality."

It's not about the money. That may be the comment from today that I'll remember most.

———

I've shopped and sampled farmers markets all over the world, but I am an amateur compared to my friend Nina Planck, at whose side I am presently strolling. Nina is a farmer's daughter, founder of markets in London and Washington, D.C., and former boss of the market program in New York City. She's also an author of *Real Food: What to Eat and Why*, advocate for traditional foods, and conscientious omnivore. Nobody knows more about this stuff, believe me. She is one of my foodie heroes.

We're far from the city, at a market on the New Jersey–Pennsylvania border, not far from the Lambertville–New Hope mecca of genteel semi-rural living. It's the middle of summer, too, and a gorgeous day—farmers market nirvana.

"This is a place that invites you to linger," Nina says, "and the activities they bring are relevant and good. So, today is tomato tasting with dishes made by the soup guy. And I was here recently for dairy day, and there's free ice cream then. Also, a number of other dairy demonstrations. Pennsylvania, obviously at one time, and still to some degree, was a heavy dairy region."

"What's it like here in December and January?" I ask.

"The dairy people are here," Nina says. "The fruits and vegetables that can be stored are here, and the meat people, and of course coffee and baked goods. I don't think they shut down completely at any point."

"Even if it's cold, people will come?"

"That's right. The quality of apples in storage is so much higher now because of what they can do with humidity and gases. And then of course there are now canned peaches and canned tomatoes, canned jalapeños, all that stuff. And there's a substantial—you don't see it so much on a nice day in August—but there's a substantial meat and dairy component here, which is year-round."

"I've talked to fruit farmers," I say, "and they told me about the things they can do to just slightly process their apples and pears. For example, they discovered people will buy dried apples, so they core them, cut them up, put them through a desiccator, and sell them that way. It gets them a higher margin than just selling apples, but it also gives them something they can sell all year, and people think of them as a healthy, responsible snack for their kid's lunch box. It means that instead of just being farmers, now they're food producers. And their customers are getting local, artisanal goods from people who not so long ago were just growers."

"That's exactly right," Nina says. "And I think it's nice for us to distinguish between foods that are processed on an industrial scale and have ingredients that we can't spell or pronounce, and foods which are processed in a fairly low-tech, customary manner. Canning is a very old process. Drying, even older. Slaughter and drying meats, older still. Grain milling we've been doing for ten thousand years at least. So, if simple food-processing machines are affordable, and if state and local agriculture authorities are willing to have simple regulations and inspection standards, then it's good for everyone."

"Right," I say, "but who's actually in charge?"

"Frequently, a farmer. When I was little, we had rotating farmers managing the markets on a volunteer basis. That is not effective. You just immediately run into minor problems of self-interest, corruption, and friendship and alliances and competition, and soon they're not minor."

"Like what kind of problem?"

"Well, the chief one is fairness and competition," Nina says. "You have to treat everybody fairly, if not always exactly equally. Kind of like how you raise children. So, someone might say, 'I'm selling a lot of tomatoes here, and if you invite another tomato grower, I'm not going to sell as many.' A delicate way to handle that is to say, 'We invite you to bring *all* the produce you can grow, not just one thing.' But when

I start a new market, I am careful not to have three lamb producers and no eggs, because I don't want to start out offering my farmers a market where they're going to go home with fifty dollars instead of twelve hundred dollars. So that's very sensitive. It was called *commodity balance*, which I always thought was a terrible, Soviet-style term, but it's just the selection of vendors that is healthy for the growers, healthy for the market, and healthy for the eaters.

"So that's number one. Number two is the question of space. Here, we're in a generous area, on grass, and it's a blessing and a curse. There's no permanent infrastructure, which is nice because that's really expensive to put up and someone has to maintain it. On the other hand, it means the farmers need to bring their own tents and they need to hold them down in the wind and the rain. But because you see this nice, loose circle of vendor stands, there's no question that if I need six more inches I can have it, while at a really tight urban market that can get testy."

"What are some other things you have to deal with when running a market?"

"After competition, space, fees . . . well, the last one would be cheating. You just *know* that some guy is not actually growing the corn that he's selling. These markets are small communities and they're rife with gossip. So, you need to have farm inspections to protect the integrity of the market. In Virginia, some vendor would show up with a whole load of peaches and onions and we just *knew* they were from Georgia, because farmers can tell. Once, my father actually tailed a farmer to a place where you could buy wholesale produce in Washington, D.C.

"But you have to hand it to the farmers," she says. "*They* created these markets. They're not called farmers markets just because they sell farm produce. It's because the farmers organized them in the first place."

"The farmers were desperate to find a way to end-run the wholesale distributors and sell directly to consumers," I say.

"Exactly. And if they borrowed somebody's parking lot and did it all themselves and didn't charge the farmer-vendors, then good for them. But over time, markets mature and they have to get professional."

I ask Nina, "What else influences how these markets mature and grow?"

"Well," she says, "chefs will ask farmers to grow things for them. There's no question that chefs have been a driver in this field. And customers have been a driver, because they can come right to the table and talk to the farmer who grew their food. Our culinary habits, our ethnicities, our traditional foods at holiday times—these are all things that customers have brought to farmers. Like honey and apples at Rosh Hashanah, the Jewish New Year. We knew there weren't a lot of Jewish apple growers and beekeepers at these markets, so the customers' demand informed the farmers what to bring. Hiring immigrants to bake the breads of their cultures is how they're introduced to us. I didn't grow up with Mexican Day of the Dead bread, but I learned about it because of Latino bakers.

"And then all the other farm and food professionals. An inspector, an agricultural extension agent, the future farmers of America youth agriculture groups. All of these are slowly shifting us from the old model of agriculture from the fifties, sixties, and seventies, the way that was criticized by Farm Aid and Willie Nelson, into smaller, more regionally distinct, more sustainable, and healthier foods."

I ask, "To what degree are these markets influenced by immigrants bringing their foods in to sell?"

"It's very active in any community where there's a large number of eaters who were not born in this country," Nina says. "The markets have been slow in finding the farmers from those immigrant communities. Greenmarket, in the city, does have a program for immigrant farmers, because we wanted to get more Latino growers bringing food in."

"Where there's a big customer need."

"That's right. And also, self-employed in their own businesses. There are a lot of businesses you can run yourself and be independent. Plumbing, electricity, and farming is a good one too. In certain places, like Minneapolis–St. Paul, you have the Hmong immigrants, from Laos. They are a huge influence on the farmers markets there. So this is not recent. Any urban place where there are big African communities or Asian or Latino communities, you really see a different flavor of market. We're here near Pennsylvania Dutch country. We're looking at some dairy, some pork, some sourdough. And a lot of produce. This is not a particularly diverse market from a food culture point of view."

"I saw a kimchi stand."

"Yeah, but that's part of the fermented foods boom. It would've been cool if a bunch of Korean producers had started that. But I think that was more the traditional foods people and Brooklyn hipsters who got into fermented foods and now they're borrowing the recipes. I would say that started from a food trend rather than from a community of fermented foods people."

"At other farmers markets, I just realized, there are usually lots of smells. I'm not getting that here."

"I think you're right. One, they're not cooking very much food. The meat and the dairy products are all chilled. We're not smelling them at all. Two, the food truck today is—we'll have to look. I think maybe a crepe truck; we'll look. But sometimes it's pizza."

"It *is* pizza."

"And you're smelling a little of the wood-fired pizza. But we're in a very wide-open, grassy area with a breeze. So there goes the smell. At our London farmers markets, we have really good sausages and burgers and bison burgers. And they're delicious. And they smell great. But I hate to walk through the smoke."

"Did you ever see the old live poultry markets on Broome Street in Manhattan?" I ask. "You would go into a store and there was a wall of small cages. And you would pick the chicken you wanted, and they would take it in back and kill and pluck it and clean it and you'd go home with a fresh dinner. This was when people still raised animals for food in their backyards—chickens, ducks, rabbits."

"From the nineteen-twenties through the fifties," Nina says, "Jewish immigrants left New York City and went to Flemington, New Jersey, and became poultry farmers out there. And there are still poultry farmers from there. A couple of fellows in their sixties walked up to our house near there and said, 'May we walk around? We're cousins. And that was our grandfather's chicken farm. He had ten thousand chickens and it was our job to bring them in at night.' You can see why farmers eventually decided to put everything indoors, in cages, because bringing in ten thousand chickens every night is not easy. And they said their grandma kept her carp for gefilte fish in our waterfall, in a burlap bag. So, there's a long tradition of wanting to eat things that were raised—"

"Close to the source," I say.

"—and close to their lives."

"Nina, why do you think shoppers come here? For the same reason they would go to a fancy produce store, or is there a difference?"

"The primary reason people come is that the food tastes better," she says.

"That's the thing with farmers markets," I say, "the assumption that you're buying something from somebody who actually eats what they're selling you. I guess there's no better endorsement."

"That's it," she says. "We grow everything we sell. We eat everything we sell."

In the final analysis, we don't really *need* an open-air farmers market to find the food and drink we want. But there's something about the whole experience that goes way beyond food. You get the sense of being part of a community here—you're doing more than just restocking your kitchen. Once in a while, you may run into a neighbor or an acquaintance in the aisles of your supermarket, but here it's different. First, we're all out in the open air, all doing the same thing, acquiring what we need to live. When we see what other people have bought, we may do the same, after asking them how exactly they prepare rapini. The assumption, I think, is that people shopping here use what they buy to make wholesome meals—food that's good for the body but also for the planet. We reinforce one another's good habits and social consciousness just by being here. You get the satisfaction of knowing that your money is going directly into the pockets of the people who nurtured and nourished your food to life. There are intangibles present at the farmers market that do not exist anywhere else in our food environment. There's romance. There's theater. There's dirt—clean dirt. It all adds up to . . . to *something*.

In the end, I believe, that something—whatever it is—is the main reason we love farmers markets. Amen.

THREE

The Supermarket of Virtue

Okay, where were we? Right, back at the supermarket entrance. Let's step inside and take in the view.

All right, stop. Look around.

I know what you're thinking: *Why are we staring at produce? That only proves how good somebody is at their job.* You don't even realize that you're being dazzled by a garden of earthly delights.

Look up a second. I want you to notice the lighting. Spotlights are positioned so they'll shine down just so on the fruits and vegetables. It's the kind of lighting movie stars used to demand in their contracts. It's designed to make anything look beautiful and dramatic. Even broccoli.

Now, pay attention to the black backdrops behind the produce. The dark color makes everything pop. The tomatoes look like rubies. The limes look like emeralds. The eggplants look like . . . hmm, I can't think of a big purple jewel, but they're gorgeous, aren't they? Notice the perfect glow on those apples. It's no accident. Look over there, at the fine, cool mist, like early-morning dew, falling gently over the parsley and the Swiss chard and the kale. Now, ask yourself: Why would produce that was picked more than a week ago and then transported thousands of miles inside a tractor-trailer suddenly need to be misty? It's part of the seduction, and we're the ones being seduced.

There's no category of retail environment that relies on total sensory stimulation more than where we're standing right now. You may walk into a candle shop, or the Armani boutique, or Burger King and think your senses of sight and smell are being excited like nowhere else. But you'd be wrong. It's just as true here, amid the turnips and the squash.

In fact, before we even reached this point, as soon as we walked in the door and turned to the right (since that's the direction we all automatically turn, possibly because most of us are right-handed), we entered into sensory overload. Okay, maybe not overload exactly, but definitely an entire zone of calculated sensuality.

It started when we stepped into that field of fresh flowers. This section is a fairly recent addition to supermarkets, but it caught on fast. Practically every food store now sells flowers and plants, and usually close to the entrance. In mild weather, they might even be displayed outside. You could say it makes sense that flowers are sold near produce, but that's not why they're here.

Also up front, near the flowers and the produce, is where we'll usually find the supermarket's olfactory powerhouse, its secret weapon—the in-store bakery. The air here is warm and perfumed with every kind of bread, cake, cookie, and pie, and maybe the aroma of hot coffee too. Once, the only bread that supermarkets sold was white, sliced, and in plastic bags. If you wanted anything more exotic, you went elsewhere. Now you can find your Wonder Bread *and* your artisanal sourdough cranberry-walnut loaves all in the same store (though completely separated, of course). But even if this bakery section never sold a single crumb, it would be doing its job.

The reason flowers, bakery, and produce are often together and right inside the entrance is simple: Good smells mess with our brains. They relax our inhibitions and ease our resistance. All this freshness fills our heads with subliminal messages. Our olfactory nerves are being stoked by the green, vegetal signal of produce and flowers, the Proustian nostalgia of sweet comfort foods baking in ovens. We all feel the close connection between smell and taste—when our noses detect the presence of something we love to eat, the aroma makes us salivate, and we suddenly desire it like crazy. But here it goes deeper than that: Smelling good things relaxes our mental discipline. It makes us more susceptible to the blandishments that are everywhere in a store selling food.

In short, it makes us buy more stuff than we need.

Store designers, architects, supermarket managers all know this. Hence the presence of this powerhouse trio—flowers, bakery, and produce—right inside the entrance. Think of it as foreplay.

I asked my friend Kevin Kelley. He's a partner in Shook Kelley, an international design and strategy consulting firm. Kevin is a trained architect who has worked all over the world on everything from vast urban environments to supermarkets to individual products.

"We believe that smells are one of the most powerful senses, and we try to activate them in specific ways in the store," he said. "While creating smells that are appetizing to the stomach is important, we also like to use smells and sounds to associate the brand with deeper emotions. For instance, we use the smell of cinnamon rolls around the holidays to tap into the nostalgic, *Miracle on Thirty-Fourth Street* side of customers. And we use the scent of baby powder to trigger their parenting side. We're not doing this only to gin up sales, but to get people into a mind-set where they will enjoy their time in the store more."

He continued, "We find that smells are so covert and hidden in the psyche, people aren't always aware that an idea is being introduced in their head from a smell. Whereas the eyes tend to be more conscious. We definitely use the produce section and floral as a kick-start. It helps a lot in communicating freshness and putting customers in a good mood. We have also been trying herb garden walls and 'living walls' in the store to help with smells, visuals, and even touch."

Increasing our enjoyment of the time we spend here. It sounds like an odd goal, but it links to a bedrock principle of retail: the longer shoppers remain in a store, the more they'll buy. We'd all prefer to get in and out of the supermarket as quickly as possible—this isn't really where we want to spend a leisurely hour wandering the aisles. But the store needs to slow us down. If we leave here buying only what we planned to purchase—only the items on our list—then this environment has failed miserably in its main mission: to inspire us to buy more than we intended.

Even if we consider the grocer's tricks of the trade sneaky, is there any harm if they get us to buy more fruits and vegetables? Or is it possible for produce to look *too* good? Consider that, according to our research, we fail to eat about 20 percent of the fresh fruits and vegetables we buy. Instead, they rot in our refrigerators until into the garbage they go. Buying produce is a lot like buying books—sometimes, what we're really purchasing is a fantasy: tonight, instead of watching TV, I'm going to read; instead of ordering a pizza or nuking some frozen burritos, I'm going to buy that beautiful zucchini and make the recipe I saw online.

Read any good books lately?

I throw out gorgeous fruit way too often. I love figs and can't resist buying them, despite their hefty price tag. Half the time, I end up tossing them. In the store, they look like they came from an Old Master still life. Then I get them home and find they're tasteless. I wonder if that has any connection to the fact that they're packaged in boxes of twelve and sealed in clear plastic, meaning I can look, but I can't buy one or two to make sure they're ripe and tasty.

I feel guilty for throwing my figs away, but not guilty enough to eat lousy fruit. We all enjoy the bounty of American foodways—maybe a little too much. My lovely Turkish wife has finally taught me that dried figs are much more reliable and consistently delicious.

We've always thought of the United States as an agricultural colossus, "breadbasket to the world," as the saying goes, home to amber waves of grain and et cetera. And yet more than half of the produce we see here today was grown in foreign countries, mostly Latin America and Canada. And that will only increase. According to the U.S. Department of Agriculture, by 2030 about three-quarters of the fruits and vegetables we eat will be grown in soil other than our own.

That's partly due to the ways in which our expectations of the produce section have changed. Once, we ate only the things that were in season. When they were out of season, we did without. In this way, even we city dwellers remained in touch with nature's rhythms. No more.

Here's an example: Do we really need fresh blueberries year-round? In my neighborhood fancy grocer, I found them from three different countries—Peru, Chile, and the United States. Interesting to note that the domestic ones were also the most expensive, which may partly account for the popularity of imported produce. Why can't I accept what every human being since the dawn of time has known—that produce is seasonal, and blueberries don't grow near me all twelve months? I should just enjoy them while I can. Barring that, I could always buy frozen. I can find wild blueberries from Maine that were picked and quickly frozen in season, meaning they also required less transportation to reach me, and so I would be doing the planet a little favor too.

Instead, I'll probably buy the imported ones. I love blueberries.

Young eaters may never even realize that growing seasons are a thing. Why would they, when they've never had to deal with that reality? It's like their relationship with what's now known as "appointment TV"—the idea that a TV program comes on at a certain day and time, so you must be in front of your set to watch it. Streaming and DVRs made that concept obsolete, as archaic as . . . seasonal produce.

Globalism plays a big part in the international bazaar that is the current-day produce section. We never ate many avocados or papayas before we were introduced to them by migrants from Mexico and Central America. Now we can't get enough. Our new appetite for these and other newish (to us) fruits and vegetables might represent a plus in the health column. But those crops are grown almost exclusively outside the United States, usually in the tropics. Some fruits—bananas, limes, pineapples—are virtually all imported. Over 80 percent of avocados we eat are imports. Even those blueberries, which grow here in abundance—around 57 percent of them are now grown elsewhere.

Due to market forces, government rules about importing foreign produce relaxed. We used to be fearful of invasive plant species from abroad causing us problems. We also worried about how foreign farmers used pesticides. I think the perceived benefits of globalism and free trade have quieted (or suffocated) those fears.

Look around now and notice how the produce here is packaged and displayed. For most of the twelve thousand or so years of agriculture's existence, fruits and vegetables were traded as naked as nature made them. They come equipped with their own skins and peels and shells, after all, and that had always been enough. But if you look around, you'll see that things are no longer so simple.

Most of what we see here today is still being sold un-packaged, in the raw. Aside from the obvious economic reasons for selling produce as is, there's an aesthetic consideration, at a time when we want our food to be as natural as possible. Again, the subliminal signaling. Today, supermarkets boast about produce they sell that's "local" (without specifying what exactly that means), and it's displayed as though the farmer just dropped it off. The popularity of farmers markets, where the clean dirt of the field still clings to the garlic bulbs, speaks to our desire for fruits and vegetables unprotected by plastic and shrink-wrap. And we're all now sensitized to the carbon footprint of food packaging, and to the futility of recycling, which, it turns out, doesn't really save as much of the planet as we were led to believe.

Look up ahead, at those sweet potatoes on display in the cardboard box in which they were shipped, a bit of anti-chic chic—a sure sign that they must be fresh, so fresh the store didn't stop to unpack them. I'm always amazed by how un-squeamish we American food shoppers are when it comes to how we buy produce. Look at that couple there, standing side by side, touching practically every peach in the bin, hefting them, examining the skins for blemishes or bruises or cuts, making sure there are no weird dents or bumps or other imperfections. I figure between them they touched about three pounds' worth and ended up putting four peaches (the only ones that passed inspection) into their cart. We shoppers all feel free to paw and palpate the pears and beets and eggplants and everything else until we find the most perfectly smooth and firm (but not too!), beautifully shaped and colored specimens. Does it ever occur to us that all day long other shoppers have been fondling that same produce? And so, whatever we choose is guaranteed to have been serially groped by strangers of unknown hygienic habits? And yet we don't seem bothered enough to insist on more packaging.

Once, it was the grocer's job to select the produce you and your family would eat. You asked and they picked. If you bought a pound of tomatoes, there were bound to be a couple of weird ones in the bag. It was the sensibly democratic way of making sure we didn't waste any food just because it was a little on the ugly side. Now? Are you in the habit of intentionally choosing a couple misshapen oranges to go along with the rest? Probably not. Where does all that homely, slightly dented, off-colored produce go? Don't ask. Farmers, produce shippers, and grocers know better than to ask us to eat it. Try going to an open-air market in Europe and picking out your own produce. That's a good way to earn a sharp slap on the hand.

Now throw a viral pandemic into the mix. The science seemed to go back and forth about whether COVID could be transmitted via surfaces. We knew it traveled through our exhalations. Would consumers demand more packaging, not less? And on everything, even here in the produce department?

And what about all those supermarket salad bars, where you could scoop up your own imported olives, marinated mushrooms, stuffed cherry peppers, and other delicacies from open containers? And the steam tables of prepared foods? They all disappeared at the outset of the pandemic. They're already back.

I have yet to see a store where shoppers are now forbidden to touch anything they wish. For all the fear, dread, and anxiety we felt, we were soon as blithely confident in our continual good luck as ever. Was this solely because the science indicated that catching the virus from surfaces was unlikely? Or was it just American optimism and the resilience of human habits? Beats me.

I'm struck by the fact that our produce sections have become so splendid, and our tastes so sophisticated, and yet the store exerts so little effort in selling us. No matter how spectacular the selection and variety, or how beautiful the displays, the routine is still the same old—it's our job to grab a plastic bag, throw in our plums or radishes, and then be on our way.

How would I make it different?

The retail transaction was revolutionized not long ago by two innovative companies. In its stores, Apple did away with traditional counters and put the salesperson and customer side by side, at tables. The emotional vibe of the interaction went immediately from adversarial to collaborative—from someone trying to sell you a phone or a computer to someone trying to help you choose the right device for your needs. It didn't even feel like a sale any longer (until you saw the bill). The French cosmetics chain Sephora configured its shops to do essentially the same thing. You and the sales associate are like best friends now, searching together for the products that will make you even more beautiful.

How might this work in a produce department? You could start with an associate wearing a big green apron, roaming the aisles, greeting shoppers, offering assistance and advice. I can't count the number of times I've encountered a fruit or vegetable I've never seen before and wondered: What the heck is this, what does it taste like, and what do you do with it? I'm an adventurous eater, but even I hesitate to buy something that's a total mystery.

Often, if a fellow shopper is buying something that's unfamiliar to me, I'll just ask, "Hey, what is this thing? How do you cook it? What do you serve it with? How does it taste?" Invariably, I get an extremely friendly, helpful response—people love sharing what they know, especially when it comes to food. I've learned a lot about cooking from the volunteer tutors I enlist in supermarket produce departments. It's always fun. But it's totally ad hoc. Not every shopper is as shameless as I am.

Compare the supermarket experience to how produce is sold at farmers markets, where we can discuss our choices with the person who grew them—always a source of good, useful, frequently fascinating information.

One day I was at my local outdoor market and saw a drab-looking root vegetable with an intriguing name: watermelon radish. Because I'm a sucker for weird produce, I asked the vendor what it was and what to do with it. If you've yet to try one, it tastes nothing like a watermelon, but under that dun-colored exterior is a brilliant, gorgeous, hot pink–orange interior—"the Cinderella vegetable," as I've seen it described. A week later I saw it again, this time at an elegant café, shredded in a salad. It's firm, crisp, and slightly sweet, and is my culinary discovery of the century (so far). Usually, I cut it into slices and eat it in place of crackers, with cheese or dips, meaning I've eliminated some refined grains from my diet. A definite plus.

In the rest of the store, there's packaging to tell us everything we need to know—ingredients, calories, nutritional information, cooking instructions, and more. We are completely informed about our Oreo cookies and instant mashed potatoes and ketchup and hot dogs. But nothing about the crucifers, the legumes, the tubers, the leafy greens, the berries, the dragon fruit and starfruit and kiwi fruit, and so on and so forth, here in produce. I know these strawberries are good for me, but how good, exactly? What is it they contain that makes them healthier than Froot Loops?

Instead, we get nothing. Only perhaps a price tag.

If only there were a produce sommelier, someone with a nice smile and serious practical knowledge of how to make fruits and vegetables delicious. They might have recipe handouts to make life a little easier, or links to YouTube instructional videos. They could offer coupons, which would make shoppers even more likely to engage. Not long ago I saw a video about an easy way to peel butternut squash. Now it's one of my go-to dishes. That never would have happened without that click. Supermarkets could install monitors dedicated to tutorials on how to choose and prepare vegetables and fruits. I guarantee that shoppers, younger ones especially, would make use of them. The store could also just display QR codes, so consumers could watch a video on their phones and take the lesson home with the spaghetti squash they just bought for the first time.

In some posh markets, I've seen "vegetable butcher" counters—places where you can take the produce you just bought to be cleaned, peeled, chopped, sliced, diced, cubed, minced, julienned, or anything else you desire, by an expert knife wielder. People appreciate anything that makes fresh-food prep easier.

"Sommelier" may seem like a highfalutin job title for somebody who shows you how to choose the perfect papaya. But if you're like most people, you spend a whole lot more money on fruits and vegetables than you do on vintage wines.

This would also be a place to connect the in-store experience with the messages we get in the outside world. We hear lots of talk about how we need to shift to a more whole-food, plant-based diet, for our own health and that of the environment. But it's mostly talk and not much action. We're constantly bombarded with well-meaning dietary advice from various governmental agencies and organizations, but it doesn't seem to have much influence over how we eat. Maybe it takes the profit motive to bring about real change.

Will we love our carrots or grapes better if they lose their anonymity, if we see the dirt where they grew up and the kindly farmer who planted and nurtured them for us? I think we might.

We've also become more aware of the environmental and ethical implications of our food choices. Not just how the food is grown and whether it is done using toxic chemical agents. But also the impact of transporting it thousands of miles, as is the case with lots of produce, and all the plastic packaging required to keep food fresh and shoppers reassured. And whether the people who grow and harvest our food on far-off continents are being treated fairly by our standards.

So much concern centers on food because it is here that we can make a difference. We can't refuse to patronize giant utilities and industries that contribute mightily to the planet's degradation. We consume electricity and gasoline at such a scale that even if we wanted to cut back, we wouldn't know where to start.

But in the supermarket—here we feel we can make a difference. That one plastic clamshell, that single case of bottled water, that cocoa harvested thousands of miles away, those local apples. Someday, all produce will be labeled with information about its carbon footprint—how many miles it traveled to reach us and what toll that took on the environment.

Hey, look over there—it's perhaps the most striking use of new technology currently found in supermarkets: the smiling robot gliding around the store. Its developers gave it big googly eyes, to render it friendly looking and harmless to shoppers. It performs just one function: it can detect a spill on the floor and alert the store's maintenance staff. That's it. Not exactly the highest use of cutting-edge twenty-first-century tech you've ever seen, is it? Maybe it's a stalking horse—the harmless electronic harbinger of more sophisticated robots to come. What will they do when they get here? Stock shelves? Detect shoplifters? Pass out food samples and coupons? Will they scan all your purchases and charge your credit card? That would be helpful. Or will they sneak items into your cart? We'll find out soon enough.

———

As we continue along the periphery of the store, we're moving from plants to animals. Now we'll deal with issues of ethics along with everything else. Questions of health too.

Okay, here's dairy. The sale of milk itself has been in steady, steep decline for years now. When's the last time you heard any medical expert telling us to drink three big glasses a day? That was always more marketing than nutritional science, but when it worked, it really worked. And so, when planning supermarkets, the conventional wisdom was always to stock milk in the corner farthest from the entrance, forcing shoppers to traverse the entire store, since everybody needed milk *all the time*. It just shows how hidebound supermarkets are that milk is still found there, even when its attraction has clearly soured.

Smart store designers are now experimenting with new tricks to get us back to this corner, according to my architect pal Kevin Kelley. "In terms of *where* we put the bakery," he says, "we have tried a mix of options—up front, on the side, et cetera—but one of the most effective things we've seen is putting that smell, particularly cinnamon rolls, in the back of the store, which pulls people through." Especially in food stores, we'll follow our noses anywhere.

For years, I've suggested supermarkets move milk all the way up front, just inside the entrance, so shoppers who need it and nothing more can run in, grab some, then split—thereby making it even easier than it is in convenience stores. In fact, the rise of convenience stores is largely due to the ease with which we can buy a few staples like milk, bread, eggs, and beer and then be on our way.

Have stores taken my savvy advice? Let me ask you—when's the last time you saw milk displayed up front?

Dairy has seen the same explosion in variety as the rest of the food environment. Where once there was whole milk and skim, now there's a long list of choices. In trendier markets it's possible to buy un-homogenized milk, thereby charging shoppers more for a product that's cheaper to produce. Grass-fed dairy—whether milk, cheese, yogurt, or butter—may be scarcely healthier than the conventional kind, but it sounds better, and that's good enough for us.

The biggest driver in this section seems to be the multitude of yogurts now available. Once, it was strictly for health nuts and the small minority accustomed to the cuisines of the Balkans. It's still health food, but take a look at all the sugar-infused variations: yogurt with sprinkles, with cookie bits, with M&M's. It's obvious by the packaging that these confections are aimed squarely at children. Doesn't bode so well for the future, does it?

This is also where all the alt milks—the nondairy products made from nuts, hemp, oats, soy, et cetera—can be found. All plant based, meaning in direct competition with everything else in this section. For obvious reason, the dairy farmers hate these imposters. They fought even the legal right to use the word "milk" on anything that doesn't come from a cow or a goat. A losing battle. Traditional dairy is going to continue being squeezed by ethical eaters on one side and health-conscious ones on the other.

Okay, let's move on. To the best of my knowledge, nobody has figured out a way to inject sugar or candy into eggs. But the explosion in choices has struck here too. Let's stand back a minute and watch that young guy scanning the shelves.

Eggs once were the very soul of wholesome nutrition, the first food of the day. We knew they were healthy because they contained everything needed to create new life. Their inviolate nature is so deeply held in our consciousness that their badness and goodness became metaphorical, as in the old-school Britishisms "He's a bad egg," or "a good egg," or, for the last one into the pool, "a rotten egg!"

That guy shopping is attempting to decipher the language of egg cartons. He's got his work cut out for him. There are the traditional, generic eggs with no further description on their white Styrofoam containers. This almost surely means the hens were held in the unimaginably cruel conditions the egg industry is known for—trapped in too-small cages, beaks severed, just total, relentless, heartbreaking misery. These are the cheapest eggs, no surprise. Depending on the amount of time this fellow has spent reading about the conditions under which eggs are produced, he may be blissfully unaware that buying the cheapest eggs underwrites such unspeakable cruelty. Maybe his budget doesn't allow him to care.

Now he's examining the recyclable packaging of "cage-free" eggs, which sounds better, although it's possible to keep chickens uncaged but still in less than humane conditions. Next to those are the "free-range" eggs, another great labeling term that's just as vague and non-committal as "cage-free." I see another brand that proclaims its eggs to be "all-natural," which is equally meaningless—what's an unnatural egg? One label boasts that its chickens are given "vegetarian" feed, which is a shame since the natural diet for these birds includes insects, worms, grubs, and small rodents. I once saw a carton boasting that its eggs were "gluten-free," a safe bet since gluten is the protein contained in grains and nowhere else.

Now he's squinting up at the top shelf, eyeing "pastured eggs," which at least means something specific and somewhat verifiable. How so? This brand includes, on the carton, a QR code that, once scanned, allows us to see a short video of the farm and all its happy, freewheeling chickens. But *how* can we be sure those chickens laid these eggs? We can't. Even transparency has its limitations. These, of course, are the most expensive eggs—the ones from hens raised as they always were, before they were turned into living industrial machinery.

All those distinctions contribute to the egg's story—its narrative. Are you going to choose a cruelty egg? Or does your involvement in your breakfast's story line extend to the captive animal that produced it for you? Those of us who will spend more money in order to prevent chicken misery should be praised and imitated. But I wish somebody would come up with standard labeling rules, to make it a little easier to be a good egg.

Meanwhile, this poor guy is still going back and forth among all the possibilities. He's too young to remember when buying eggs was a simple task, before every choice came with moral baggage. He's now texting somebody, probably asking for advice, or to see if they really do need eggs at all.

Meat next. Oh boy.

If supermarkets were serious about tickling our senses to increase sales, there would be somebody here in the meat section frying bacon all the time. I think that aroma rivals warm bread and hot coffee for its impact on the human salivary glands and shopping cart. That's the thing about burning animal flesh—it connects to something way deep and primitive in our brains.

And yet supermarkets steer clear of any such appeals.

This is the section of the store where transparency and narrative have yet to catch on, and they never will—for obvious reasons. "Transparency" here only refers to the plastic wrap that seals what's for sale, keeping it all at a safe distance. We won't catch an errant whiff of blood or flesh or skin. We definitely will not see videos of all this meat when it was still on the hoof, back on the farm; nor will we be treated to the sights and sounds of the slaughterhouse or meatpacking plant.

Is there a more problematic locale in all of retail? Even gun shops look good in comparison. Here is where animal cruelty meets environmental destruction meets unhealthy nutrition, if you believe the research that says we eat too much animal-based food. Of course, none of this does much to inhibit those of us who eat meat. In fact, we consume more than ever, per capita. The current popularity of keto and low-carb diets has driven many of us to consume more meat, not less. But even here, the emphasis is increasingly on meat raised naturally—

without hormones or antibiotics, fed grass instead of grain—which often also means animals treated humanely (right up to the moment they're slaughtered and butchered, of course).

Like I said, this territory is ethically and nutritionally shaky ground.

Before the supermarket drove the neighborhood butcher shop into extinction, you might come across an actual animal carcass, or at least a portion of one, in the process of being carved up for home consumption. That was a sign of honesty as well as freshness—we were being shown the precise source of the meat we would feed our families.

In places like Brooklyn and Portland and other outposts of neo-artisanal foodstuffs, such displays still exist. But practically nowhere else. I recently visited a small non-chain supermarket in a suburban neighborhood where many recent arrivals from Latin America live and shop. There, the meat was on full display so that shoppers could inspect it closely before they bought, as they no doubt always have. I saw a large aluminum tray filled with bloodred chicken hearts, $3 a pound, a great bargain for animal protein.

Would that display work in the supermarket we're currently touring? I don't think so.

———

Killing and butchering animals on the scale required to feed a meat-hungry world has always been a challenge. It's no coincidence that one of the greatest works of muckraking journalism centered on the meat industry. Upton Sinclair's 1906 novel *The Jungle* was a turning point, though not in the way he intended. His aim was to expose the terrible working conditions for the poor immigrants who toiled in the meatpacking industry in America's cities. Readers were more outraged by the filthy, disease-ridden conditions under which their food was being rendered. As a result, the federal Meat Inspection Act was passed. "I aimed at the public's heart," Sinclair said, "and by accident I hit it in the stomach." More than a century after his book was published, our sympathies still don't extend to the men and women who keep the meat section of the supermarket constantly stocked.

As we saw in dairy, the innovation in meat departments today is in non-meat—the various plant-based substitutes that are still growing in popularity. They all imitate ground beef and sausages at this point, but there's no reason to think that, as the technology improves, we won't find thick slabs of non-meat as red-blooded (thanks to the beets in the mix) as any rib eye or porterhouse. And can plant-based pork shoulders, chicken breasts, lamb chops, and hickory-smoked bacon be far behind? The impetus behind non-meat is partly health-related but mainly millennial revulsion at the conventional meat industry. As with eggs and dairy, it comes down to this question: Are you willing to pay more than necessary in order to spare those animals (and the environment) further pain and suffering? If you're trying to feed a family on a tight budget, it becomes a lot easier to pretend ignorance about where all this meat and poultry comes from.

There are lots of high-tech start-ups trying to make lab-grown meat commercially desirable, and I have no doubt that some will succeed. This development would be not just a simulation of animal protein but . . . but what? We're getting into the realm of Frankenmeat now. It's costlier than the real thing, too, at least at the outset. Scientists can already "grow" something meat-like, but the trick will be creating products that look, feel, smell, and taste enough like meat to replace it, and do it at a price competitive with whatever a pound of ground beef will go for at your local supermarket or fast-food joint.

Here we are now, at the tail end of the supermarket's periphery, the seafood department. Appropriately bookended with produce—the two sections of the store that now function as our favorite over-the-counter pharmacies, so touted are these two foods as natural medications. A steady diet of berries and salmon is all we need, or so the scientific literature informs us.

Once more, my friend Kevin Kelley had an interesting insight.

"This area is more of a negative concern," Kevin says. "While consumers want to know that the fish is fresh, the window of time we have on freshness is so short. We find consumers can be merciless if there is a fishy smell, so we focus more on the sound of chunking ice machines and having an employee water down the area with a hose while wearing big rubber boots. Again, we have no science on this except our observations, but we find that the senses are competing for the dominant voice or influence in the consumer's head. While smell may be a factor in seafood, if another sense—like hearing the sound of ice being made—is bigger, it will win out over the smell."

In a prototype Carrefour market we worked on in São Paulo, Brazil, the fish section had a band of chopped ice around the display case, and some strategically placed fishnets. Like everywhere else in the supermarket, a little theater goes a long way.

And with that, we've reached the end of the supermarket perimeter. Now we can enter the funhouse—the rest of the store. But first, a little detour.

FOUR

Yes, We Have Bananas

Bananas are my favorite fruit, because they have appeal.

And not just *my* favorite—they are the world's most popular fruit. Only tomatoes—which are also fruit, botanically speaking, though we eat them as vegetables—sell more. But bananas are king. We go through over 153 million tons a year if you include plantains, which are bananas too.

Did you know that bananas are actually a kind of berry? Weird but true. In the wild, they have seeds, which we would probably see as a turnoff had they not been bred out. The number-one source globally is India, which produces over 30 million tons a year. That's around three times as much as the number-two producer, China. They only grow in tropical climates, meaning mostly in Asia, Africa, and Latin America. You may have noticed—there are no bananas at farmers markets. Nearly all the bananas we get in the United States are from Mexico or Central and South America.

Where I grew up in Southeast Asia, we had many varieties, many colors and sizes. One of my favorites was large and green when ripe and tasted like lemon custard pudding. The only place I've been able to buy it in New York City is in Chinatown.

Here, we eat mostly the beautiful bright-yellow-skinned Cavendish variety, bred for taste and color but also for durability. The fruit inside is tender and must be protected during its long journey by that tough peel.

Health-conscious eaters know that bananas contain potassium, which we need, although there are plenty of other foods containing more: spinach, mushrooms, sweet potatoes. Interesting thing about potassium: everything that contains it emits radiation. But not much. When we eat one banana, we receive four hundred times less than we get on a coast-to-coast flight.

Bananas can be baked into bread, of course, and also show up in banana beer and banana wine, both of which I hope to try someday. Mostly, though, we eat them just as they grow. And that's all I have to say about bananas—for now.

———

When you're traveling through northwest Arkansas, you can nearly always be sure of one thing: your destination will have some connection to the largest buyer (and seller) of produce on the planet, also thought to be the largest buyer and seller of organic produce anywhere, which might suggest some kind of high-end purveyor of healthy, costly eating.

We're going to Walmart.

It's hard to have a career in retail and not have an opinion about Walmart. They are either a huge success story or a voracious monster. The first time I went to Bentonville, where Walmart is headquartered, my motel room cost $28 a night and came with a hot breakfast. My first evening there, alone at a bar, I met the town undertaker.

The company's main offices were distinctly plain. My reception was polite, and I got the feeling that while my clients didn't agree with everything I suggested, they listened. When I read about founder Sam Walton, I liked that he identified his imaginary customer as a single mother trying to raise her children.

Over the years I've worked for Walmart, I've watched them grow, learn, and mature. Bentonville today is a small but very cosmopolitan city. Crystal Bridges, their museum of American art, is world-class. The transformation of the city is in the best traditions of New Urbanism, and the company has done a remarkable job of harvesting the best and brightest workers from their international divisions and integrating them into the home office. Are there flaws and legitimate criticisms? Yes. But I have been converted into a fan. In the context in which the company works, and the scale at which it must play, it deserves more credit than blame. I can remember ten years ago when the head engineer for Walmart stood in front of their board and said that for every dollar they gave him to spend on energy conservation, he would return a dollar in savings within thirteen months. That engineer, Charles Zimmerman, was my first hero at Walmart.

We're in the company of another stellar Walmart executive, Victor Verlage, whose title is "senior director of resilient sourcing." Victor is driving. I'm riding shotgun, asking questions. We're headed to a Walmart food distribution center, one of forty-five such facilities across the United States, each of which is essentially a warehouse for all food headed to Walmart stores. Each center services around one hundred locations, for the forty-five hundred or so (at this writing) Walmarts from sea to shining sea and of course in Alaska and Hawaii too.

It's telling that so many people I know are surprised to learn Walmart sells groceries, especially fresh produce. It says a lot about the self-contained bubbles we all occupy. If you live in a major city, you have almost certainly never bought a grape or a carrot from Walmart.

"Victor," I begin by asking, "where did your life in produce start?".

"In Mexico, on a row crop farm with cattle and an agave plantation," he says. "I managed the vegetables for my family. Then I got an invitation to run a greenhouse project called NatureSweet. You've probably seen the yellow plastic bowls full of snacking tomatoes. I moved to the West Coast, and I helped them with the greenhouses, managed them for a while, and then I was in charge of building new clusters and setting them up."

"How did it feel going from working for the family to working for a corporation? Was there a sense of liberation or—"

"Well, it was a big disappointment for my family. Because we were always raised to be in the business. And making that decision was not easy for me, but I figured, you know what—business-wise we were doing fine, but professionally I was stuck. The climate on Mexico's Gulf Coast does not lend itself to any kind of technology modifications to farming, and here was an opportunity to manage and build greenhouses, which is my passion. And I decided, you know what, 'I'm sorry, my family, but I'm going to go ahead and do this.' My dad didn't speak to me for about a year. He was really, really upset. *Really* upset. But you know, we moved on."

"Okay, at the risk of showing my ignorance, what is a row crop?"

"That means soybean, corn, grain sorghum, cotton, stuff like that. Those are commodities, not produce. The land in that part of the world is not very fertile, and there is little water. Agave lends itself well to poor soil and drought. And then on the better soil, we planted grow crops. But on the best, *best* soil, we grew produce—vegetables. All open field. And the best technology we could bring at the time was drip irrigation from Israel. This is 1986 or so. It was a fun stage."

"Is your father proud of you now?"

"He's proud of all of us. You know, what can you say about your children, right? We all love them and we're very proud of what they accomplish. And so, even though I was a black sheep for a while, after years went by he recognized that I had made the right move for me and my family. He endorses it now."

"Do you think you'll go back someday?"

"So, here's the deal. As you know, Mexico's got some issues, some instability and safety issues. Unfortunately, our farm is in between two cartels fighting for control, so it's unsafe right now. My wife is an architect from Texas A&M. She built our house, and she designed and built our house there on the farm. The plan had always been that we would finish our professional careers here in the States and then retire in our house back in Tampico, Mexico. But that's no longer a possibility because of the security issues. So, we've changed plans, and now we live here outside of town on a little farm."

"And you grow here?"

"Yeah."

"This gets us to one of the topics I'm very interested in," I say, "which is that small-scale agriculture is now an acceptable profession."

"Correct. It's becoming trendy again."

At my farmers market, I meet couples from non-farming backgrounds who have chosen to go into the business. Because there's no middleman, it's economically viable. There's an organization in New York that helps immigrants set up small-scale farms using a very limited amount of space. And with some basic language skills and a little training, it's a viable business that can support an extended family.

"We need a lot of people who understand how to leverage technology to grow food," Victor says. "In a nutshell, we all know that it has not been cool to be a farmer for many years. There's a romance attached to the idea of being a farmer, but it's hard work for low pay, so nobody actually wants to farm. And so, we lost a lot of farmers. Until now. Partly because of all the advances in technology, suddenly farming looks attractive and cool to smart young people. Now a lot of them *want* to be farmers. In the past fifteen to twenty years, we have had major developments in growing food in controlled environments—vertical farming, greenhouse farming. But we still don't have enough people who know how to grow food that way."

Believe it or not, leading the way for inexperienced farmers using cutting-edge technology has been an outlaw segment of the agriculture community: cannabis growers.

"They showed the way with indoor growing," Victor says. "What the cannabis growers did, when it was still illegal—in the basements of houses—was figure out how to use artificial light to grow a crop. There are two big indoor farming conventions every year in the U.S. And half is dedicated to growing food, and half is dedicated to cannabis. So, I go there and start meeting people, and the ones who really, *really* knew their stuff were the pot growers. Because they've been doing it for so many years, right? It's just out of the closet now. The guys who were trying to grow food were still trying to figure things out. Cannabis is actually attracting a lot of the talent that we had growing food in greenhouses around the States and in Canada. It's booming.

"But what's interesting is that all this innovation, the breakthroughs that have happened over the past five or six years, is laying the foundation for how we'll feed the world in fifty years. Because we will have many more mouths to feed. Nine and a half to ten billion people by 2050. And by then, fewer resources and very erratic, changing weather. Somehow, we need to find technological solutions to deal with it. Indoor farming is not going to be the solution for everything, but it will lay the foundations of how we grow food in the future, inside *and* outside. That's exciting. So, if you look ahead, it will be more attractive to exponentiate what we can do. If I have one acre of vertical farm, depending on the crop—let's talk about lettuces and herbs, because that's what we're growing in controlled environments, leafy greens and herbs. That's how we're learning. Using the square footage of a vertical farm, I can grow many more times biomass than I can growing in a field. I can take a warehouse that's, say, thirty-four or thirty-six feet high, and I can stack a layer of lettuce growing every three feet, all the way up to the ceiling. You do the math. All on the same size footprint. And I can continually harvest that lettuce and reuse the space every thirty-five days.

"Now try growing that same lettuce in an open field. It's one layer only, so you need a lot of land, and you're exposed to the climate, to all the uncontrollable conditions. A lot of retailers and food service people are now migrating their supply chains to controlled environments. There are already cases established all over the world where many crops are being grown indoors. In Japan, a perfect melon, with the vine attached, in a wooden box lined with velvet, is an appropriate gift to bring to someone. They are all now grown in greenhouses. You couldn't grow as many in the same space outdoors as you can in a greenhouse. And outdoors, maybe one in a hundred will be perfect enough. I went to Japan to see how they do it, and they get ninety percent perfect melons."

"Warehouse" doesn't really do justice to the place where we're headed, for the simple reason that fruits and vegetables aren't like other products. Produce is perishable. It's fragile. It must be kept at a certain temperature. That's the unique thing about food supply chains—they rely on speed and timing. And mistakes are expensive. This illustrates another reason why companies find it so attractive to manufacture ultra-processed foods: the profit motive. When you factor in transportation from the warm climates where lots of produce grows, and the cost of keeping it all cool, you understand one more reason that whole food is so expensive compared to food-like industrial products that have a shelf life of years.

"It's very important to us that we flow the food through here as fast as we can and not age it ourselves," Victor says. "Each fruit or vegetable has its own innate shelf life. There are some that will last three months; there are some that will last three days. And in that time frame, you have to give the customer the biggest portion of that life span possible. We are now concentrating not on shelf life but on home life—how long the produce will remain fresh in the customer's home.

"So, we need to build food systems that extend the home life of each one of these items, so that they are more and more relevant to the customer. We have certain levers we can pull. We have DNA. And we have varietals. We have growing systems. And then we have to do a good job with the part that you will see today. You're going to look at the last third of the supply chain. First it must be grown. Then transported. But in this last third, if we're not careful, we can use up all of the value of the product before it reaches the customer. And this would be due to inefficiency in our system."

"And that's completely a function of how quickly you get produce to the store, right?" I ask.

"Yeah. There are some varietals that will last longer than others. It is a function of how and where you grow the food. We have a video of two tomatoes, same variety, harvested the same day, but one was grown in the field and the other in a greenhouse, and you can watch them age, and the greenhouse tomatoes last thirty to forty percent longer. Because they grew under the right conditions, with no stress at any time."

"But do they taste the same?"

"No," Victor says. "You can actually make the greenhouse variety taste even *better*. I told you that my previous life was spent building and operating greenhouses in Mexico. The tomato was our vehicle. Our project was to build a brand and a relationship with the customer, to build trust and loyalty. And we had the levers to make that tomato more flavorful just by the way you fertilize it and grow it. And that's just one example. We can do that with everything. So, it's all about the variety, and how you grow it, and how close to market you can grow it, and then what the supermarket system does to keep it fresh."

"Victor, today when you go into a store, you can find fruit and vegetables that were grown all over the world. Am I right in thinking that makes the challenges even greater?"

"Remember," he says, "that the United States market, over the last fifty years, has been built around one thing: having the permanent presence of every kind of produce at all times of year. There are places in the world where they eat food only in season. In Argentina, they don't eat peaches out of season. But in the U.S. and in Europe, they expect to find everything fifty-two weeks a year. We have trained customers to expect that they will find a watermelon regardless of the season or the weather. A grape, the same. An orange, the same. Because of that expectation, we now have to source our fruit and vegetables from all over the world. If we don't, our competition does. Some produce comes from areas that are easier to manage than others. But some are very challenging.

"A good example of that is cantaloupes. Cantaloupe is a category that since 2000 has been dying. Per capita consumption back in 2000 in the U.S. was around 11.7 pounds a year. Now it's 7.6. And it consistently goes lower and lower. There's a good reason for that. You have to spend at least $3, which many people don't have, to bring some pleasure to your family. And then you get it home and it's not so good and you end up throwing it away. It's cardboard. So why would you spend your money on that when you have mandarins and grapes and a lot of other alternatives? And therefore, cantaloupe is in decline."

Before I ask Victor the logical question—why are cantaloupes cardboard?—we should acknowledge something interesting about the fruits and vegetables we eat: they're all in competition with one another. If one is somehow made better tasting, then it will likely result in higher sales—at the expense of the others. Because we can eat only so much fruit. What can we do to make an apple, or a grape, more popular? Most often, the answer is to make it sweeter. That has a lot to do with our consumption of high-calorie treats—we've taught our taste buds to favor sweetness over other tastes. The latest star of the grape family is one that tastes exactly like cotton candy. There are several new varieties of apple that are significantly sweeter than their forebears. And does the banana's global popularity have anything to do with the fact that each one contains one hundred calories or so of sugar? (By point of comparison, two bananas are roughly the same as a Hershey bar, from a calorie perspective.)

So, the scientists use the tools at their disposal—the levers, as Victor calls them—to alter the plants. Breeding new varietals. Growing plants in different ways, in controlled settings far different from our mental picture of vast green fields and dense orchards.

Victor and his counterparts elsewhere have a very particular relationship with produce, one quite a bit different from ours. When they look at a fruit or a vegetable, they ask: "What do consumers expect of this thing?" What do we demand of a pineapple? A plum? A peach? A raspberry? All very different expectations, and so each fruit's story is unique. That's really what Victor is looking for—a better way to tell the stories. Okay, let's get back to my cantaloupe question.

"Victor," I say, "why is it cardboard?"

"It's cardboard because it was bred and grown to ship. Especially in the wintertime. It is grown in Central America and Mexico, and it's bred to put on a boat and hold up through the supply chain and look good in the supermarket."

"But it's impossible to do all that and make it taste good?"

"It *is* possible. We're doing it. We're actually— We have proprietary rights to a variety that we've developed in collaboration with Bayer. And we've brought it to market. You'll find it in the stores." (It's called the Sweet Spark.)

"Bayer the aspirin company?"

"Yes."

For a time, Bayer, the German pharmaceutical maker, also owned seed companies, and Walmart worked with them to develop a variety of cantaloupe. Today, Walmart owns the seed concern, and so the cantaloupe itself.

"Yeah, it's what we're trying to fix, category by category, but cantaloupe is one that I'm more passionate about, because I've been working on it for six years now, to fix it, and I—"

"Wait a second. Victor, you've been working on a cantaloupe for *six years?*"

"Longer! My very first dollar I ever made as a farmer was from cantaloupes. I made good money growing cantaloupes back in 1986. My passion is melons. This is a fun story. This was for my thesis at Texas A&M. At the time, people made money in what they call 'marketing windows'—meaning the time period when you can sell a particular fruit. The farmer would aim for a window, and so if you could get to market two or three weeks before everybody else, you made your money right there, okay?

"My thesis was to study twenty-five different commodities over twenty-five years and identify if there were marketing windows that could be leveraged to make money. Back in '86, cantaloupes were nonexistent between Thanksgiving and Christmas. You couldn't find them in stores. So, if you had cantaloupes during that period, you were guaranteed to make money. My breakeven was twelve dollars a box, and I sold every single box I grew for the first three years for thirty-seven dollars. Thirty-seven dollars! It was robbery, man. We made a killing. Now, what held the market back in the late eighties was that the demand was institutional only. It was sold for the salad bars that needed to have cantaloupe in there. For a restaurant to pay five dollars for a cantaloupe is no big deal. For a housewife it was a different story.

"And what happened was all of my farming neighbors saw that I was making money, so *everybody* planted cantaloupes and we saturated the market."

"Victor, you killed the market!"

"Yes. But by that time, I had made my money for three years, so it didn't matter. But let's go back to cantaloupes in Walmart. What Walmart is doing, category by category, is trying to understand what drives consumption, and what creates satisfaction, for each one of these products. What is this fruit or vegetable used for, what do people expect from it? In a cantaloupe, there are attributes that are desired but are going unmet. A cantaloupe has to have a certain degree of softness, but it has to be flavorful. And since flavor is what drives sales, we commissioned a study from an academic institution to help us understand, chemically, what it is about the flavor of a cantaloupe that pleases the palate."

"And what did you learn?"

"Well, there is not one profile that pleases everybody; we understand that. But if we can have a cantaloupe with four or five natural chemical components that please seventy percent of the population's palates, that's a home run. So, based on that research, I can tell you that if you like cantaloupe, really what you like is sucrose. Not glucose, not fructose. It is the sucrose that pleases your palate—that and isobutyl acetate, and five other acetates. And if you have those chemical components in the fruit, seventy percent of the people will say, 'I love it.' *Done.*

"So, that's our challenge, to take every one of those categories and make it truly relevant. Tomatoes, grapes, citrus, melons . . . everything. One by one."

Relevant produce! The man is a philosopher.

"Victor, when you use the word 'relevant,' do you mean make it into something that people will want to eat? Something that tastes right?"

"Make it relevant to whatever the average consumer expects out of it. I'm going to give you another example. In tomatoes, we segmented the market into eight different uses. Some people buy a tomato to snack. There is a list of attributes that particular tomato needs. It has to be bite-sized. It has to be sweet, which means it has to have the right chemical profile. Remember, all this is natural. We're not touching anything GMO. This is all conventional plant breeding. You know, just using what Mother Nature produces for us. Wholesome.

"For that snacking tomato, flavor is the main driver. But we also do a great business with Roma tomatoes, which are used mostly for salsa. The value proposition there is price, period. Size doesn't matter; color doesn't matter. It all matters, of course, but people buy the Roma to make salsa. It's the base. The texture is what matters most. The chunkiness. The flavor in salsa comes from the pepper and garlic and onion. It doesn't matter so much if the tomato itself doesn't taste so great.

"And when we saw that, we hit a home run. We can buy Roma tomatoes cheap and sell them for a very low price and it becomes a great item."

"You also mean relevant specifically for Walmart shoppers, as opposed to Whole Foods shoppers, or—"

"Yes. It's customer demographics. It's obviously easier to make money if your consumer will pay five dollars for a cantaloupe than if your consumer can only afford a dollar or two. Our job here is to democratize healthy food that tastes great."

And with that, we've arrived at our destination, the distribution center through which all food sold in the region must pass. From the outside, a typically bland, tranquil corporate campus.

Inside, amazing. Vast, as you might expect. Ceilings around forty feet high. Steel shelving all the way up, packed with everything edible you can think of, from bottled water to Cheez-Its to fresh fruits and vegetables. There's one room in here that's as damp as a rain forest (94 percent humidity), thanks to misters, and cold as a winter day (34 degrees Fahrenheit), to keep the leafy vegetables damp and cool. Forklifts are zooming all over the place. Drivers are wearing wireless headsets, filling orders to be loaded onto trailers that will make their way to the stores. To a visitor it looks chaotic and a little scary, but nobody crashes or even comes close. Still, you walk near the walls to stay out of the way. Chad Clubb, the manager of Quality Control Operations, is our guide. He and his team are responsible for inspecting and approving all the fruits and vegetables that pass through this building on to Walmart stores.

"What time does your day start?" I ask him.

"Mine starts at two a.m.," he says. "And on a good day we might be able to get out between twelve thirty and one p.m. On a not-so-good day we might be here until close to three."

"Did you ever think in high school that you would end up doing what you do?" I ask him.

"No," he says, laughing. "I started at the bottom. I started out pushing carts into the building, cleaning the restrooms, and—you know, twenty-eight years later I'm the quality control manager."

I said at the start of this chapter that we might not be finished talking about bananas. Turns out I was right—the first stop on our tour is the banana room.

"Bananas are the jewel of the crown," Victor says.

" 'The jewel,' meaning . . . ?" I ask.

"The most important category in our business. By volume *and* by value."

In a year, Walmart sells over 1.5 billion—*billion*—pounds of bananas. It's the entire company's best-selling product, which possibly makes it the best-selling item in all of retail on the entire planet. Bananas!

"And if I don't do it right, I hear about it," Chad says. "This distribution center services our home office, not the best position to be in." He laughs. "Everybody's got their eyes on my fruit, my vegetables, everything. So, if anyone's going to be critiqued, it's going to be me. That's how it is."

The banana room holds roughly one trailer load at a time, nearly one thousand cases. Here is where Chad undertakes the precise maneuvers required to get bananas to the stores at exactly the right moment. Too green and no one will want them. Too ripe and even if shoppers do buy them, they'll quickly turn overripe at home. Maybe even inedible, depending on how you like your bananas, leading you to toss them (unless you're a fan of banana bread) and start buying them elsewhere. Which, of course, would make Walmart unhappy.

Chad's job is made even trickier because he must prepare the correct quantity of shopper-ready bananas every day for one hundred or so stores. That means he has to predict how many each store will need, which depends partly on how many it still has from the day before.

Chad has two main tools—two levers—at his disposal. One is temperature. He can quicken the ripening by making the banana room warmer, or slow it by cooling them down. The other lever is a gas, ethylene. He can place bananas in tall, sealed spaces and pump in ethylene to ripen the fruit more quickly.

I realize how scary that sounds, gassing bananas. But that's only until you learn that the gas we're talking about, ethylene, is produced by a banana naturally as it ripens. All fruit, in fact, emits ethylene—it comes from a natural plant hormone that influences growth. It's why if you want an avocado to ripen faster, you put it in a paper bag with a banana and close it tight.

"So," I ask, "when they come in, bananas are bright green?"

"Yes," Chad says, "they come in at what's called stage two—green, hard, full of latex."

That "latex" is a plant protein that's chemically similar to rubber. It looks and feels like rubber, and you can see why nobody would want it in their bananas.

He leads us deeper into the banana room.

"Okay, now these are going to stores tomorrow. And this is a stage three, which means, if you've noticed, we're starting to see some yellow on the skin. But I don't know it's a three until I cut into it," which he does, with a pocketknife. "Look, the latex is not running out of it. It's already absorbed all of that. And if you notice, the pulp is turning an amber color, the color that we want to see inside a banana when we take a bite. But that white part you see is still going to be kind of cottony. Not very good to bite into right now. I'm also looking at how the peel comes right off that banana. By stage three it doesn't get hung up or break off. If it's a stage two, that peel will snap off, just like that.

"At stage three, the peel will completely separate. That's when I start looking at the color on the outside. At three and a quarter, we'll have a little more yellow. A three and a half, your two sides will definitely be yellow, and the green on the front and the back will be a lot lighter. Turning a different shade. If I ship out a three and a half during the winter, when it gets to the stores it should be a stage four, or four and a half, because we bag it and wrap it and then we ship it. That bag will protect it against the cold temperatures on the trailer."

"When I buy them, is that the stage they'll be—a four or four and a half?"

"Well," says Chad, "that's what they *should* be. But a lot of times what you'll see at the store is a mix, okay? So, you may be seeing a solid four, which will be a little greener than most people want to eat. But then as they sit during the day—once they hit stage three, they ripen five times faster than before. And if they're in a box or a bag, they continue to heat up. Now they'll produce their own ethylene and their own heat. So that ripening process is still going on whether they're in my aging rooms or not."

And what happens when you guess wrong?

Chad steps away and points to a pallet off to the side. "These right here are organic bananas," he says. "These were pulled this morning because this is too ripe a color to ship to the stores. We had two hundred and eighty-eight cases ready to be shipped to our stores yesterday, but they only needed two hundred and fifty."

"What happens to the produce that doesn't go to stores?"

"Right now we're loading them onto a truck that's going to food donations. There are two churches here in town that take it. And then we also donate to a food bank."

"Chad, how many bananas do you eat personally a week?"

"I don't eat any."

"None?"

"No. I'm just not interested in bananas."

"What fruit do you eat?"

"I like some apples. I like stone fruit. Not crazy about strawberries because they're a pain to inspect when we have problems. That's kind of how I judge it. If I'm out there inspecting, I'm going to eat some, because I need to know what they taste like. My wife will buy bananas, but I don't eat them."

By now Chad's workday is nearly over, so Victor and I head back to the car and get on the road again.

"What the industry wants today," Victor says, "what my customer wants, is transparency. They want to trust that what I'm putting in their house is good, is wholesome, and was produced right. So, we have teamed up with IBM to go through block chain and give instantaneous transparency. It's already happening with mixed salads and spinach and strawberries. The moment the customer touches anything, it's all registered, she can know exactly where it was harvested, when it was harvested, who brought it here; all of the information is right there. Through a smart label or QR code or a Shazam hologram, my consumer can go to the store and see all that history and see a video of the farmer saying, 'I grew this with Walmart for you.' It's happening. *It's coming.*

"And the consumer can go further from there, like with a deep dive into recipes. But you have to have transparency in the entire supply chain so that everybody's happy with what they're bringing home."

"Victor," I say, "given that people have such great access to online information, is this technology how you're going to bridge the distance between us shoppers and the source of our food?"

"Well," he says, "in today's world you can sit in your living room and order almost anything you want. Right to your doorstep. So why should you get up and drive ten miles to— Ninety percent of the U.S. population lives within ten miles of a Walmart. That's a fact. So, how do we entice shoppers to drive through traffic and come to the store and enjoy the visit? And that's what we're trying to figure out. We call that retailtainment."

"What are you going to do to make that happen?" I ask.

"Okay, I'm going to go ahead and say this, because it's going to come out shortly. Let's pretend that you went to our parking lot, and right outside the store is a farm producing your lettuce. And your kids got to see it, and they got to—you know, even harvest your own produce. Is that a value?"

He's talking about what we imagined back in the supermarket parking lot. "I think this is the most underused resource that Walmart has," I say, "the lots that surround the buildings."

"Okay," he says, "and here, shortly, in Alaska, we're going to have a farm growing your salad in the middle of a blizzard."

"Sounds good."

"And we'll learn from that. And if to serve remote communities, and bring them freshness and flavor and fun, and healthy eating, means we turn decommissioned shipping containers into farms, so be it."

"It's bringing your product to your market rather than waiting for your market to come to you."

"Correct."

———

Victor has since been named a senior vice president at 80 Acres Farms, which creates indoor farms around the country.

FIVE

Coffee Break

Ready for a nice chemical stimulant? I sure am.

Thirty years ago, when I opened my first office, the coffee choices in our neighborhood were limited. There was a deli down the block with a pot they made in the morning and served until it ran out, no matter how long that took. If you got there early, it was drinkable. By midafternoon you took your chances. The thought that hours-old coffee might not be at its best didn't occur to the proprietors. They only made more when the pot was empty. People were less picky about coffee then. If it sucked, you made a joke about it, and then you drank it.

There was also a coffee cart down on the corner. It was one of those quilted aluminum jobs on wheels with enough room inside for a person, a coffeemaker, and an assortment of bagels, bialys, and buttered rolls. His prices were cheaper than the deli's, and he poured faster, owing to the line of desk jockeys either freezing during winter or sweltering during summer or just in a hurry to get to work. But by three or four o'clock he had left—his day started ungodly early, predawn, so he was gone when we needed him most, like right now.

At some point, I broke down and bought a coffeemaker for the office. I guess we had milk and sugar, and probably stirrers too. Most small businesses, I suspect, took pretty much the same approach. It didn't occur to anybody that your employer was supposed to provide you with free food and drink.

And that was coffee back in the olden days. No frills. Nothing fancy. Primitive, in retrospect.

Can we blame one corporation alone for all that has come since? I don't think so. We must have been thirsting for something different than we were getting, something transcendent, something like a revolution in the world of what was then and still is now essentially hot water that's been passed through roasted, pulverized seeds found inside a certain species of berry. (They're not even *beans*—they just look like them.)

If you're a fan of old black-and-white movies, you'll have seen coffee shop culture as it once existed, or at least was depicted—usually late at night, and in the presence of hard-boiled men and women hunched over white china mugs. Edward Hopper's painting *Nighthawks* made the scene iconic—four Americans and two coffee urns. So, the setup has always been with us.

But of course, now we want something more than mere coffee. We want, oh . . . let's step outside first and see what's immediately available to us. Within three blocks we find:

An old-school Korean deli with a big stainless-steel coffee urn.

An even older-school Jewish luncheonette with a sense of humor (the sign on the door says: "Sorry! We're open") and coffee the way Ma or maybe Grandma used to make it.

A French bakery.

A Belgian bakery.

A Danish bakery—in fact, according to the sign outside, "Denmark's favorite all-day Danish bakery."

An indie coffee shop, where the lights are low, the music is chill, and the staff's skin art and hair fashions are memorable.

Or, moving on, inside a clothing store, Club Monaco, in a quiet little antechamber, off to one side. The coffee shop here is called Ralph's, which sounds like your basic old-school establishment until you realize that Ralph's last name is Lauren and he owns this store, too, and this is his idealized vision of how we might have consumed coffee half a century or so ago.

"The theory with our coffee," says the friendly woman armed with a tablet who runs the place, "is that when they were first picking the blend, he was there and he picked this particular blend, his roast. So, this *is* Ralph's roast."

Or at the Godiva Café, where coffee's kick is supplemented by fancy chocolates. Or at the freestanding coffee kiosk on the traffic island, or . . . look, I could keep going like this all day, discovering new coffee opportunities. There might even be a Starbucks someplace around here. Clearly, there's something more profound going on than mere caffeination. The socioeconomic factors behind that trend, which have existed for a couple decades by now, don't bear any further explanation by me. We already know them all: the search for the "third place," the friendly locale that's neither home nor work; the gig economy that pushed so many people, especially young ones, out of the office and into the street, in search of a perch.

Even bigger picture, it's part of something that's been called the global coffee cult, a phenomenon that has sprung up independently all over the world, with its own set of aesthetics, rules, codes, beliefs, and values. The food scholar Fabio Parasecoli, writing with Mateusz

Halawa, calls it "global Brooklyn"—an "emergent cultural formation around eating and drinking." In their 2019 essay "Eating and Drinking in Global Brooklyn," published in the scholarly journal *Food, Culture & Society*, they write:

> We have observed it in cafes, restaurants, and stores, and identified it in reports from collaborators in cities worldwide, including New York City, Montreal, Berlin, Warsaw, Rome, Bologna, Rio de Janeiro, Bangalore, Bangkok, and Mumbai. . . . The roasting and the brewing, which are a spectacle in themselves, embrace the organoleptic [involving the sense organs] characteristics of Third Wave coffee [the movement that thinks of it as a high-quality, artisanal food]. . . . As baristas participate in tastings, or "cuppings," they proliferate complex vocabularies describing taste profiles that are appreciated by the connoisseurs but not the popular palate. "I'll have the Ethiopian," goes a typical order. . . . These young coffee enthusiasts talk taste with the sophistication and a sense of belonging which the Western bourgeoisie have historically reserved for wine. There exists also an unarticulated list of no-nos, which makes an appearance when someone uninitiated shows up.

(If you want to know more, check out their book, *Global Brooklyn: Designing Food Experiences in World Cities*.)

We may not all be up to that level of exquisite refinement, but it's true, coffee is now one of those products that you can consume like a tycoon even if you're broke. In luxury goods, fragrance occupies this spot. You may not be able to swing a $5,000 Tom Ford suit or a $10,000 Chanel bracelet, but for less than $100 you can buy into the legend by wearing their perfume. Maybe you can't drive the best car in the world, or vacation in the best hotel, but almost anyone can afford the best coffee the planet can manage. Funny to think it was once just a drink called joe.

Recently, I went out for coffee with two colleagues, both part of the younger generation who turned coffee from a drink into a fetish. Caffeine sophisticates—"snobs," to use another word. They're so deeply immersed in coffee—so totally dunked, you could say—that I promised not to use their names, and they promised to speak frankly.

We settle in, and the coffee talk flows.

"I never in my life thought I would pay for a Starbucks coffee ever again," says the drinker I'll call Joe. "And I was accustomed to my beautiful homemade cappuccino that I would take as my subway coping mechanism. Some people read on the subway; I like to have a cappuccino and stare into space. Now, because Starbucks, you know, has a good real estate team, there's one right at my subway entrance. There are a dozen other coffee shops in my neighborhood, but they're in the opposite direction. I go to Starbucks most of the time. And I hate myself every day because it's overpriced."

"How much are you spending?" I ask.

"Like four or five dollars a day."

"Okay," I say.

"For a shitty coffee that makes me look like an asshole."

"But you're doing it because it takes you a millisecond."

"Yeah."

"Have you ever been to a McCafé—the McDonald's version of Starbucks?" I ask them.

"I have been to one in China," says the drinker I'll call Jane.

"Yeah?"

"But that kind of also brings me back to the whole Starbucks effect," she says. "You know, when I'm there on business, I go to the McCafé in Shanghai, which was originally the biggest in the world until the one in Chicago opened. And I did get that sense of, like, it's my little piece of America here. And when you are in Shanghai and by yourself for three weeks, and the only people you talk to are your translator and the hotel concierge, it makes a difference."

The McCafé is in shopping malls all over the world. My first experience was in Brazil. The perception of McDonald's in emerging markets is very different than in the United States. Often, it beat Starbucks in entry to the market.

"Well," I say, "the best coffee that I drink is the coffee that I make myself every day."

"Yeah, tell me about it," says Joe. "I just brought back twelve pounds of beans from Tanzania."

"Wow."

"I do a pour-over," he says. "Sometimes I do a little cardamom, a little Zanzibar cinnamon in there. It's really getting me through the winter."

"I haven't gotten there yet," says Jane. "I have about four different coffee machines and I just haven't gotten the right cup."

"Wait," I say. "You have four different coffee machines in your kitchen?"

"Yeah, I have an espresso machine, I have a filtered drip, I have a French press, and I have . . . there's one more. Oh, the *other* espresso one! You know, the one that goes on the stovetop."

"But which one do you use?"

"What I use depends on the mood. It was espresso for about four years, but this last year I've actually bought my own beans and—"

"Four years! That was a long mood."

"And I just thought, one day, it was just, like, maybe it's time for a new machine. And that was my excuse. And I stopped using the espresso machine. All these crazy pods. And now I'm moving over to my drip, but it's not something that I'm going to say I'm fully enjoying."

"'Drip' means . . . ?"

"You just grind the beans and put the coffee into the filter."

"That's a pour-over," says Joe.

"Okay, a pour-over."

"A pour-over is good," he says. "If you do it right, that's the best way to make coffee."

"But I just haven't gotten there yet for myself."

"It takes some skill to understand."

"With four different machines."

"Yes," Joe says. "First you've got to let the coffee bloom, and then wait; that's the hard part."

"And then there's my French press," says Jane, "which for the life of me I have no patience for. Someone wants to come over and take it, you're more than welcome."

"No, you don't have to wait," says Joe. "This is a common misconception."

"Whatever. You can have it if you want. I'm over it."

Joe says, "I also have a La Pavoni espresso machine that I would never have purchased but was sitting in my girlfriend's dad's garage for twenty years, unused."

"So now you have three," I say.

"He got this thing in the seventies for like fourteen hundred dollars. And I refurbished it. He was going to throw it away. And it's beautiful, brass, and makes—*pulls*—a great shot. But again, that's only when I'm having a really leisurely, elaborate weekend breakfast."

"Jesus," I say. "Fourteen hundred dollars!"

"But now I mostly use my AeroPress, which is an awesome device designed by the same guy who invented the Aerobie, the Frisbee with the hole in it. These are this guy's two great claims to fame. A Frisbee that goes really far, and a really awesome, economical coffeemaker that sits on top of your mug and is, you know—it's this little cylinder that you put grounds in and you spin it around, full immersion, ten seconds, *boom*. And you can get close to an espresso or an Americano or something a little thinner if you want."

"Price point?" Jane asks.

"Thirty dollars. You should get one."

"Send me the link."

There's an unintended, I think, consequence of coffee culture that's worth noting. The number-one source of calories in the American diet today is grain-based desserts—cakes, cookies, donuts, pies, and so on. Second on the list is bread. These are the least healthy things we eat. A related fact is that young adults—the target audience for coffee culture—eat more frequently than their older or younger compatriots. And a good deal of that eating, of course, is done outside the home.

So, if I were a killjoy, I might argue that coffee is like the Trojan horse that makes our overconsumption of sweet and delicious foods inevitable.

But I won't. Ever tried Demerara sugar? Maybe you should.

Drink up! As soon as you're done, we're moving on.

SIX

The Supermarket of Vice

Okay, so now we've done the supermarket's parking lot and its perimeter. Glad to be away from so much wholesomeness? Me too. Now we get into the good stuff—the belly of the beast, so to speak.

Hang on a sec; my phone is trying to tell me something . . . wait . . . holy cow, the brand of coffee I usually buy? According to this text, today it's two pounds for the price of one. And . . . apparently there's a new variety of chunky, spicy salsa I might want to try. Hmm . . . Hey, look at the video screen on our shopping cart—there's that perky Rachael Ray, chirping from her test kitchen, "Hey, Paco, you know that organic almond butter your family loves? Today, just for you, half off the big jar!"

Isn't this how your shopping trips start? Maybe not yet, but soon, trust me. As soon as you enter the store—maybe even before you walk in, maybe even while driving there—you'll start getting pinged on your phone. Modern tracking technology makes this easy. The store will already have your complete shopping history stashed away in the cloud somewhere.

Once we're in the store, electronic smart shelving will use low-frequency radio signals and Bluetooth to know when we're about to pass any given aisle. That's when we'll get messaged some more. As we approach dairy, here's a coupon for the brand of milk we usually buy. Once we're in produce, we hear about a special deal on white asparagus, which we've bought several times in the past year. As we pass the condiments aisle, our phone informs us that our refrigerator said we need ketchup. And we yelled at Alexa the other day to remind us we need hamburgers, and because it's a Friday in summer, we'll get a blast saying that for the next fifteen minutes the store brand of frozen patties will be BOGO.

Our supermarket knows who we are, what we eat, when we shop, which brands we prefer, what offers we respond to. Did we immediately buy the new kind of low-fat Greek yogurt? Do we always stock up on whatever brand of paper towels is on sale? Are we suckers for the "10 boxes of couscous for $10" special? All that information and more will go into memory maw, and the app will put it to good use every time we even think about food.

A lot of this technology is already up and running. In the spice aisle, you pick up something you've never tried, scan the QR code on the jar with your camera, and up pops a video starring a helpful chef from the company's test kitchen, with recipes for half a dozen dishes for dinner tonight, all making liberal use of this herb and maybe one or two more. QR codes have come a long way from their origins—developed in the nineties to allow Japanese car factories to keep track of parts. Once our phones were able to read the codes, they became able to handle everything from credit card payments to directing us to websites, videos, endless streams of information about the products we were thinking about buying.

Your phone might never shut up.

Some of us—me included—will tire of these intrusions. But lots of other people will be cool with it, will welcome the blasts and take advantage of the pings. We hear a lot about concerns when it comes to the personal information that businesses collect without our even knowing. But lots of shoppers seem not to care, as long as they get something in exchange for their loss of privacy. Like bargains. And visits from Rachael Ray.

Look around. Where we're standing right now? This was ground zero during the pandemic. The reason was obvious: this is the place you go to buy stuff that tastes good and never goes bad. During dangerous times—during any times—it's comfort food, sustenance not just for our bodies but for our emotional needs. Macaroni and cheese in a box, soup in a can, jelly in a jar, sliced white bread in a plastic bag, are you beginning to see a pattern here? This is the same section we head to right before a blizzard hits, or a hurricane that's promising power outages. When we feel threatened by circumstances beyond our control, we flock to center store. Americans still have a pioneer gene—we feel safer with a stocked pantry. It's like a savings account. Yet how often in the past century has our access to the supermarket been blocked for more than a day?

In center store we find our history as twentieth-century consumers, the legacy of brands and advertising that drove network TV and print media for fifty-plus years. Here are the celebrities of American foodstuffs, the household names, the superstars. Tony the Tiger. Betty Crocker. Famous Amos. Cap'n Crunch. Chef Boyardee. Little Debbie. This was once the home of Aunt Jemima and Uncle Ben, too, and if you're still asking whether the supermarket reflects the culture at large, you're not paying attention.

This was the site of our first romance with convenience that was sold to us as sophistication. Think about the time when the TV dinner was a treat and Pop-Tarts were special. Shoppers who grew up on Ovaltine and Pepsi and Lunchables and Cheez Whiz (and Cheez Doodles and Cheez-Its) find that while much of life has changed, these dependable delicacies have not.

There are plenty of nontoxic food moments in these aisles—canned oysters and mackerel, olive oil and vinegar, rice and beans, coffee and tea, salt and pepper, honey, spices. But who in their right mind buys canned asparagus, which even sounds nightmarish, when the fresh variety is but a few paces away? This section of the store is mainly where we go for the latest advances in the science (or is it art?) of food engineering—essentially, taking real foods (grains, fruit, vegetables, legumes, eggs, nuts, seeds), breaking them down, stripping them of anything beneficial (fiber, vitamins, minerals), and then reconstituting and reinventing them as "food," which we define as anything we stick in our mouths, chew, and swallow. Because a great many of those groceries would not have been recognized as *food* in any but our most recent days on this planet.

It's not even a stretch to say that the center store of your friendly neighborhood supermarket is aggressively, directly responsible for most of the preventable chronic diseases—cardiovascular ailments, hypertension, type 2 diabetes, fatty liver, several kinds of cancer—that kill us so efficiently nowadays.

Be all that as it may, I still like center store. It's where the creativity of the food trade is on display. How much ingenuity does it take to sell lettuce? Who doesn't already know that garlic can prolong your life? But look at all the varieties of Oreos! They don't grow on trees.

I have a very personal love for center store because it's where I go to find . . . ginger jelly.

The spring of 1986 was a dark time for me. I had made fifty presentations for a new company I was trying to launch and got not one taker. My girlfriend kept helpfully pointing out that I was thirty-four years old and going nowhere fast.

I had one more pitch set up, a total do-or-die moment. I drove my battered Dodge Aries, which I had inherited from an uncle, to the appointment with a prospective client. I walked out of that meeting with a contract for a quarter-million dollars' worth of research work. A corner had been turned—not just for my company but for my life.

A few days later I was shopping at my local supermarket. Rolling my cart around the store, I wandered into the jelly and jam aisle. Something caught my eye: imported ginger preserves, $7 a jar. As a child living in Kuala Lumpur, I was sent to a British Army School, where we got traditional English breakfasts and teatimes, which always included ginger preserves—which I loved. Once I grew up, my access to this treat was intermittent. And unaffordable.

As I stood there, a thought suddenly overwhelmed me, and I started to cry. I still wonder what the other shoppers thought about the sobbing six-foot-four man blocking the peanut butter. But for the first time in my adult life, I realized, I could afford to buy anything I wanted in that supermarket. I had some money in the bank and more in the pipeline. I had always skipped the ginger jelly because it was too expensive. It went straight into my cart. To this day, you will always find ginger jelly in my fridge and backups in my pantry.

Given all the pleasures center store contains, you wouldn't think it could be a lonely place to shop. But sometimes it feels downright deserted here—like a zombie store. The shelves are full. But the shoppers are few. This is where you'll find what we call boomerang aisles— shoppers go partway down, grab what they came for, then turn back, not even bothering to see if anything interesting lies ahead. It's like we've seen it all—a thousand times. Supermarket flooring wear patterns, a good measure of foot traffic, are uneven throughout the store. Here flooring lasts longest. Fewer than 10 percent of people walking in the door go down the carbonated-beverage aisle. And does anyone go into the frozen food section just to browse?

Once we reach middle age, roughly 80 percent of our weekly supermarket buying is simply repeat purchases. We're here to replace, not explore. Once in a while, an item will drop out of our steady rotation or we'll fall in love with something new. But for the most part, we're robo-shoppers here.

It's also due to the fact that so many of the foods on display—soda, cereal, soup, cake mix—have been losing popularity for years now. You still find shelf upon shelf of soft drinks here, even though soda sales fell by one quarter from 1998 to 2015. During that same period, breakfast cereal sales fell by even more, but they still commandeer an entire aisle in most stores.

You might reasonably wonder, then: Why is so much of the store devoted to these goods? Not so long ago, the average supermarket offered around seven thousand different items for sale. Today, that number is up somewhere between thirty and forty thousand. Ask yourself, how many different things do you normally buy here in the course of a month? A hundred? Two? We humans eat around thirty different foods, according to research I've seen. Not a huge variety, considering how many edible things exist. Even if we include all the non-food items currently available in a decent-sized supermarket—frying pans, patio furniture, fireplace logs, romance novels, windup toys, windshield wiper fluid, you get the picture—we're probably being offered way more products than we really need or want.

Why might that be? Is it just that this is America and abundance is our middle name? Could be. Just as those amber waves of grain and fruited plains symbolized our natural riches, we've always been proud of the amazing splendor of our supermarkets. The array of products is so vast it's dizzying. Back in the eighties, when Soviet émigrés began arriving in the United States, we witnessed their astonishment—their *shock*—at finding supermarket shelves groaning under the weight of extravagant supply. After lifetimes of shortages and long lines, the newcomers were moved to tears by what they found here. There's a scene from the movie *Moscow on the Hudson* where the character played by Robin Williams goes into a supermarket and is so overwhelmed by the sheer number of choices that he collapses onto the floor, screaming, "Coffee! Coffee! Coffee!"

But there's another reason why center store is both exploding with choices and, at the same time, boring as hell. It's time to explain. But first, a little background.

Compared to other categories of retail, the profit margins in food are notoriously slim. In luxury goods, the markup is often 100 percent, meaning the retailer doubles the price it paid for an item before selling it to you or me. Grocers, at the other extreme, enjoy a gross margin of just 1 percent on many items, like the staples here in center store. Produce is more remunerative. Same with meat and fish. The checkout lane, bristling with magazines and candy, is the most profitable square footage in the supermarket. Here in center store, they eke it out pennies at a time. The upside of owning a supermarket is that virtually everyone who walks in the door spends money. But the profits on each individual item are small.

Because of that, grocers have come to depend on an income stream that you and I can't even see. It doesn't come out of our pockets, at least not directly. But it has a great deal of influence over how this part of the store functions—how it looks, how it is designed and merchandised. And *this* is why it's so boring.

Are you familiar with the word "planogram"? Possibly not.

It's the layout, the schematic—the *plan*—for how a supermarket (or any store) is organized. It's all the decisions about which products the store stocks (and which they don't) and what goes where. It's not architecture, but the planogram is just as important. It's like the blueprint for everything the store contains. It's complicated—but let's take a look.

My friend Ken Park is a distinguished architect who has worked on plenty of grocery stores and other projects. He tells stories about being in focus groups where shoppers say, "You mean somebody actually *designs* supermarkets?" In their minds, the stores just come into existence by default, as though someone—possibly a stock clerk, maybe a teenager with a part-time job—fills the shelves with goods in a more or less random way.

Nothing could be further from the truth. But the fact that it seems that way to shoppers tells us a lot about how supermarkets are experienced. As though they design themselves. As though they just *happen*.

But the truth is that the entire store is, in principle, carefully, meticulously planned, every product on every shelf in every aisle. And all those product placements are determined by the fact that stores charge companies for the spaces their products occupy. This is the revenue the store takes in that doesn't come from us directly (although of course the food companies cover those fees with their prices).

How are slotting fees, as these costs are known, determined? Just as you'd expect. The greater the exposure to shoppers' eyes and grasp, the higher the price. Anything at eye level costs most, because we're more likely to buy things that are easiest to find and grab as we roll down the aisles. Above eye level costs less. Below eye level, like way down under your knees, costs least. It's just like how they price tickets at Dodger Stadium—box seats behind third base cost more than the bleachers.

I have observed the slotting fee negotiations in the buying offices of chains big and small. If you are Walmart, you have the muscle. But if you're a small or regional store chain dealing with Procter & Gamble or Kraft Heinz, the power shifts to the other side of the table.

Next time you're in a supermarket, pay attention to the merchandise displayed on the very bottom shelves, down where our eyes rarely stray, where it's most awkward to browse and bend or squat and grab. That's where you'll usually find the minor players in any given category—the brands you've never heard of, the ones that don't have huge marketing budgets or major advertising presence. The ones that can't compete with the major food companies for prime shelf real estate. Shop high, shop low, is the basic mantra of savings.

But why does the planogram guarantee boring stores? A number of reasons.

First, it's why there are too many choices on supermarket shelves. In order to maximize the income that flows from product positioning— from the planogram—the store owners fill their space with stuff. They're like landlords trying hard to maximize their income by renting out every square inch of their properties. This is why there are no interruptions to the sheer walls of food in the store. No breaks just to give our eyes a rest. Think of all the inventive ways other stores have of displaying merchandise. Now imagine how a clothing boutique or an electronics store would look if they imitated supermarkets. Solid walls of packaging. Nothing on display. Deadly.

Another reason the planogram creates boring stores is that it prevents supermarkets from taking advantage of the number-one selling tool at their disposal—free samples. Stores and food manufacturers have never made much effort at this. Some food companies will pay retailers to set up sampling stations, but not most. You occasionally see a folding table with chunks of cheese on toothpicks, this week's special. Almost always from some small local foodie entrepreneur. But that's about it.

Making a real try would require a total reimagining of a store's layout. And that would mess with the planogram. But think of what the cereal aisle, or the salty snacks section, or the healthy-beverage department might be like if we could try before we buy. First, they'd be a lot more fun. Second, we'd be a lot likelier to take a chance on a new flavor, or a different brand. Sampling is 100 percent guaranteed to stimulate buying. But to do that, stores would have to forgo some income from shelf placements, and for some retailers up to one-fifth of their revenues come from slotting fees. Offering free samples of food is definitely a logistical challenge compared to letting customers try the new iPad. Whatever you offer has to be clean and safe and uncontaminated. You need staff on hand to maintain order and hygiene. To do this at multiple stations throughout center store would be a chore, no doubt.

Have you ever been to an Aldi or Lidl store? They do their own product sourcing and specialize in smaller brands, and while there are some national players, the control is in the hands of the store and the individual managers. Is there any surprise that they generate a level of customer loyalty that traditional supermarkets envy?

But more sampling would make the supermarket a more user-friendly, even entertaining, experience for shoppers. We love the idea of finding new products. Discovery is one of the joys of all shopping, in every category. Most stores are designed precisely to draw you in, to make you want to explore, to engage your brain, and to keep you on the premises. Why do you think Trader Joe's is such a popular phenomenon? Many reasons—price, their private brand foods, the overall vibe—but high on the list is the fact that they offer shoppers the chance to sample before they spend.

How exactly would that work here? Free samples in every aisle! Here, try the latest Cheerios variation! The new organic blue corn chip! This exotic grain from a faraway land! Have a cup of a soup you've never heard of in a self-heating container! Stores would see a jump in sales, no doubt. Enough to offset the lost revenue from the planogram? There's only one way to find out. But nobody wants to try.

Supermarkets remind me of another class of boring retail locales: shopping malls. And for a similar reason. Mall operators aren't retailers—they're real estate people. They lease space to retailers, whose responsibility it is to sell merchandise. As a result, malls tend to be unimaginative hulks of concrete and steel and Cinnabon. To a lesser extent, supermarkets are also more interested in renting shelf space than they are in being exciting, stimulating places to buy the things we all need to live.

And to prove my point, here we are in the condiment aisle. Take a look. Just ten mustards? Why not twenty? Why not an entire aisle, wall to wall, ceiling to floor—"Mustard! Mustard! Mustard!"

In the late twentieth century, marketers fell in love with "brand extensions"—salsa-flavored ketchup, onion and garlic chips, lemon Coke Zero. They bought more space and gave us what they thought we wanted, meaning more variety.

The ultimate irony: researchers have found that when faced with too many choices we become overwhelmed and walk away empty-handed.

Today, the byword in food retail is "curating." Shoppers want somebody to use a little discernment in deciding what we're being offered. But food manufacturers would rather treat store shelves as a real estate turf war—if you crowd out the competition, the thinking goes, you're bound to outsell them. There's even a term for it: "shelf blocking."

As a result of all that, this supermarket is constipated. It could use some relief.

Even with all the money food companies spend on shelving positions, their control over the aisles is hit-or-miss. We often photographed the shelves of a store where we conducted our research and taped the pictures to the client's conference room wall. The executives were outraged: not a single shelf followed the planogram the client had paid for. We had to explain how a supermarket really works—that once the store closes, a very tired employee restocks the shelves just before going home. And a shelf that's perfectly organized on Saturday morning will be chaos by closing time. Many of the expensive displays shipped to stores never even make it to the selling floor. They pile up in a storeroom somewhere, getting dusty, because no one bothered to remove the old displays cluttering the aisles and blocking shoppers from seeing (or grabbing) what they came for. A soft drink client reports that only one display out of three ever makes it to convenience stores' floors.

You'd think that supermarket executives and food manufacturers understand how shoppers behave, but you'd be surprised. I have spent what feels like years of my life walking clients up and down stores, trying to get them to see how customers experience the place. I used to bring a skateboard with me, and I'd invite people on my tour to sit on the board and roll up and down the aisles, just so they could see how much merchandise was, for all practical purposes, invisible and beneath the grasp of shoppers. No way old eyes and knees will allow customers to browse a shelf six inches off the floor.

Most customers, I should say. Another good use of the skateboard was to show retailers and manufacturers how the store looked to small children, who are enthusiastic shoppers, especially of cookies, cereal, and dog treats. It's a whole different store when you're three feet tall. We tell clients that the shelves must be merchandised for all customers, but it's a hard lesson to teach.

Okay, slow down. Here we are at the outlier in center store—the frozen food section. Where the healthy and the heedless exist side by side.

Plenty of junk food and borderline-unhealthy items in here. A whole section of pizza, both old-school and new (cauliflower crust, vegan cheese). Ice-cream section—it goes on and on, but vegan is possible even here, if you're willing to pay $12 a pint. Burgers—patties of every kind, from bison to turkey to vegetation, and even the entire burger: microwavable patty, bun, cheese, and all, for the truly unmotivated home chef.

At the same time, this aisle may be the healthiest source of food in the store, for the simple reason that the plain vegetables and fruits found here have been picked and then immediately frozen, before the nutrients had a chance to fade. This is my other source of blueberries. Instead of a plastic container of gemlike fresh fruit, I get a plastic bag of frozen solid. The aesthetics suffer a little, I'll admit, but it's a small price to pay. Frozen broccoli? Same deal. Frozen edamame, spinach, asparagus, kale. Same.

The pandemic brought about a new surge of popularity for frozen foods, no surprise. We were being urged to stock up enough food for at least two weeks of lockdown, which for a family of four would mean, let's see, three meals each, that's 12 meals a day plus desserts of course, times 14 days; that's . . . 168 meals on hand at all times. I can't attest that many people followed that impractical advice, but clearly a lot of us did ransack the frozen food section in those early days. There were not just shortages—the freezers were stripped bare. Total frozen food sales rose by about 25 percent during COVID spring, most of that in seafood, meat, and fruit. According to a survey conducted by the American Frozen Food Institute, almost half of respondents said that they expected to purchase "a lot" or "somewhat" more frozen food in the near future.

In our own research, we find that the most popular frozen foods are, in order:

- Ice cream
- Potatoes
- Convenience dinners (think Hungry Man)
- Breakfast (think Jimmy Dean)
- Pizza

Meanwhile, frozen vegetables make up less than 5 percent of supermarket purchases, even though—penny for penny—they're the cheapest produce in the store. Frugal people and big families know best: frozen food is where it's at. If only someone would invent glass doors that didn't fog up, making what's behind them so darn hard to see.

For all the nutritional badness to be found in center store, it is also where serious advances are being made in cutting the environmental impact—not of the food but of the containers holding it.

I've talked to veterans of the packaged foods business who say that at some point soon, nothing we see here now will be sold in boxes or cans or bottles or jars. Nothing? Hard to imagine, I know. But easy to see the advantages. Companies will be glad to see that day, assuming that whatever replaces all this packaging is cheaper. Consumers are becoming more sensitive than ever to their personal impact on the environment, and they want to do something about it. Not every shopper, maybe. But younger ones especially, which shows us where the future lies.

Just look around us right now, at every container, and imagine it out of existence, to be replaced by . . . something.

But what will take the place of all these containers? They're still figuring that part out, but all over the world, tech wizards are developing alternative, cutting-edge materials. Not substances that we'll attempt to recycle, as we do today, because it's becoming clear that recycling is a scam. It makes us feel good but requires so much energy—meaning fossil fuel—to make plastic, glass, and metal reusable that the net result doesn't do much to benefit the environment.

Will you be content to buy food sold in paper wrappers? In reusable cloth bags? That would help a little. There goes every box of cereal and cake mix (assuming those two products even survive), every big plastic tub full of sugar, and a lot more. Plastic pouches might also be a good alternative. They require a lot less material than the jugs of milk, bottles of vinegar or olive oil, cans of black beans, we use today. You'd take that product home and pour it from the pouch into a nice pitcher or bottle or some other container, or that pouch will slip into a container. The irony is we see that kind of innovation in other markets across the world. Ever buy milk at an Israeli supermarket? . . . It comes in a biodegradable bag.

Many of the really cool-sounding futuristic packaging materials are still being invented. Lots will be made from plant matter that could be repurposed at home. Boxes and bottles that you throw into your compost heap. (Wait, you don't have a compost heap? Oh, that will change too.)

The only question is whether we'll feel safe with new forms of packaging. We all want to reduce our carbon footprint—as long as it doesn't inconvenience us too much or freak us out. A few of us are old enough to remember the Tylenol poisonings of 1982, when seven people in the Chicago area died because someone (still unknown to this day) laced the pills with cyanide. Suddenly, every package became tamper-proof, and they remain so even now. Food packaging especially must inspire confidence among shoppers.

What else will happen once we remove most of the packaging from this part of the store? First, in terms of sheer weight, everything will become considerably lighter. That means manufacturing and transportation products will become less of a strain on our resources too. And the footprint on store shelves will shrink.

This is going to be a big deal, no pun intended.

Because the greatest transformation of this part of the store will be its ultimate disappearance. It's going to keep shrinking until it shrinks right out of existence. Every supermarket executive is already preparing for that day, even though it might sound inconceivable—at first—to us shoppers.

Perimeter, yes—maybe bigger and better than ever.

Center store, no. History. Gone.

Where will it go? Where it's going already: online. Let's face it, if I'm buying baked beans thirty times a year, do I really need to see them every time? How about oatmeal? Chickpeas? Crackers? Tea bags? Frozen waffles? It's crazy that we've been willing to trudge through these aisles week after week only to pick out the same products over and over again.

This shift started long before COVID, but the pandemic caused an explosion in online grocery buying. It practically became mandatory. In the first month of lockdown, March to April 2020, the number of people shopping online in the United States rose by more than 30 percent. The dollar volume went up even higher. That worked for most of us. That migration to online buying evaded the 15 percent of American households without bank accounts or credit cards. Remember this when someone tries saying food deserts are a thing of the past.

Someday, your grandchildren will marvel (or go glassy-eyed bored) at stories about how in the olden days you had to push a metal cart up and down aisles inside vast markets, choosing your own purchases, and push it all to a human being who would tell you how much to pay. And then lug everything home. Sounds inhumane, even to me.

By now, we have a multitude of ways to shop online—directly from our supermarket to pick up or have delivered, or from Amazon and all the other virtual retailers, even from the smallest, most specialized food merchants. Once you realize you can buy Amarena cherries from Italy online, it feels ridiculous to drive to a store for grape jelly. For many of us, center store already works this way—we order online, or we subscribe or just yell at Alexa, "I need flour and olive oil, quick!"—and someone will show up in about the time it takes to order a pizza.

But won't the stores suffer at this turn of events? Heck no. Suddenly, their real estate needs will shrink, along with their utility bills and staffing requirements. Supermarkets can't wait to shove us out the door.

However, there still could be a role for center store, should retailers and suppliers decide to get creative. The biggest, perhaps insurmountable drawback to online shopping is how it kills our impulse purchasing. Part of the fun of shopping is spotting something we've never bought before and tossing it into our cart. How will new products ever catch on if center store goes away? How will we even know they exist? How will the food industry ever innovate again?

Here's how: center store could become a showcase for new foods. Whenever one of the packaged goods giants—or one of the upstarts—comes up with something new, it could be introduced here. And in a way that allows us to try before we buy. This part of the store would look completely different. Better. They could even keep a modified version of the planogram, but one that allows for more creative displays and a little open space.

Will that ever happen? I'm hopeful. And doubtful.

Okay, we did the periphery of the supermarket, and now we're through with center store, meaning we're through, and we can finally get out of here—once we pay.

Uh-oh.

This is like the final insult of shopping. You've chosen to patronize this establishment above all others. You may have had an enjoyable experience choosing things you wish to own and eat or drink. There's a good chance that this will cost you a not-insignificant sum of money.

How does the store reward you? By making you stand in line and wait around just for the privilege of taking your stuff home. We're so accustomed to this stage of the process that we don't even question it, let along wonder why we don't deserve anything better.

The cashier—the cash wrap, in retail talk—is a problem no matter what kind of store we're in. It takes too long. It's poorly organized. We get bored and antsy standing there with nothing to do but silently urge the shopper in front of us to *move faster*. By now, in many supermarkets, we're our own cashiers, thanks to shop and scan, or self-checkout lines. Which doesn't necessarily move things any faster. But it gives us the sense of control—maybe the illusion of control—and it provides us with something to do besides browse through supermarket tabloids.

We're used to the idea of being volunteer employees of the businesses we patronize. Anything to save us a little time. First the banks used ATMs to turn us into tellers. Then the gas stations turned us into pump jockeys. Once e-commerce came along, our computers became stores. Then our phones became stores. And once that happened, *we* became stores, because the entire transaction, from shopping to shipping to paying, was completely in our hands.

But if you want to see how technology has revolutionized the cash wrap, you'll have to leave the country, for Western Europe, because that's where they're doing it right.

Visit a supermarket in Sweden—you pick up a cart, put your kid and handbag in the seat, and arrange the bags you have brought with you. You pick up a scanner and roll cart, kid, bags, and all onto a scale and get your starting weight. As you stroll the aisles, you pick up a product, scan it, and put it into a bag. You finish your shopping, then roll the cart onto another scale, which does the math. Then you scan your credit card and roll out the door. (The weigh-in is to make sure every purchase is paid for.)

Variations on this are found all over Western Europe, where scanning tech and public acceptance are high. The stores like it because it cuts labor costs. The shoppers like it because . . . well, because they are spared the checkout line ordeal we put up with every day.

Okay, we shopped. We bagged. We paid. We're outta here.

SEVEN

A Basil Grows in Brooklyn

We're riding the subway in Brooklyn, headed to a farm.

Once, this patch of the Bed-Stuy neighborhood was home to a windmill. In the late forties the windmill was replaced by a public housing project, Marcy Houses, famous because it's where Jay-Z and Tracy Morgan grew up. Walking from the subway tonight, we pass a kosher deli, a bodega, a hipster coffee shop, elegant new town houses, and some classic aging New York City tenements. Welcome to the melting pot.

Just up the street from Marcy looms a hulking old industrial complex, eight stories high, with loading docks and a huge parking lot out back. In 1849 the Pfizer pharmaceutical empire was founded here. Then, in 2008, Pfizer bailed on the neighborhood, and with it went six hundred jobs, which is how life goes in the global economy.

And then the building was bought in 2011 by an investment firm that specializes in repurposing old industrial sites. From the outside, it looks unchanged. Inside, on a lobby wall, is the first hint of a difference, the building's directory of tenants—homespun little placards for around a hundred small companies that now call this subdivided giant their home. Most are in the food business, outfits you'd expect to find in twenty-first-century Brooklyn, meaning natural, earnest, artisanal, focusing on doing just one small thing really, really well: Pickles. Ice cream. Soda. Chocolate. Pizza.

This is also the home of Square Roots, a Brooklyn kind of farm.

Up on the third floor, on a chilly Tuesday night in November, there's a crowd gathering for the weekly farm tour. As soon as Tobias Peggs gets here, we'll begin.

He's running late.

To keep ourselves entertained, we all mill around sampling the three herbs grown here—basil, mint, and chives—spread with locally sourced hummus on whole-grain crackers. There's also hot chocolate made with oat milk, all served up by the farm's youthful, energetic, telegenic team. If you wanted to make a sitcom about a high-tech urban farm, you'd hire them all.

Okay, he's here.

"Hello, everyone. Sorry to keep you waiting. Today is a pretty busy day on the farm. My name's Tobias. I'm the founder and the CEO—cofounder and the CEO of Square Roots. Thank you for coming. Okay. Great. Cool. So, this is what is going to happen. We're going to do a quick intro. And give a sort of high-level overview of what's going on. That will be probably the most boring part of the whole evening."

Tobias is a young, wiry, charismatic guy with a British accent and an easy, confident manner. Also telegenic—think Jude Law in sneakers and jeans. His cofounder is Kimbal Musk, brother of Elon, so clearly this place is aiming toward the future.

"Then," Tobias says, "the much more exciting bit is we're gonna go see the farm. So, our farm is outside in the parking lot. We will take you to a twenty-acre farm that is in a parking lot in the middle of Brooklyn.

"Pretty much anything you hear tonight or see tonight is on the record. Please take photos. *Please* share them on social media. Honestly, that helps us. So, I'd be very disappointed if you *didn't* do that. So, definitely get your phone out."

This is the universal winning strategy of all enterprises like this one—to turn as many human beings as possible into no-cost transmitters of commercial messages and spiritual manifestos. Today, every human with a phone is a vector of information. That may turn out to be the Internet's ultimate benefit, assuming it doesn't kill us all first. Giant global corporations attempt to harness these impulses, this energy. But they don't do it as well, as believably, as this little outpost of millennial yearning. Post photos? Try and stop me! Of everything and anything that catches my eye, of whatever seems cool or brilliant or futuristic, of the things I think you, too, should love and admire and desire.

What does Square Roots gain by turning us into volunteer content creators? Will they sell more mint if I post a photo of it on Instagram? Not enough to matter. But if enough of us post, we will boost its social media presence, the digital real estate it occupies, without which twenty-first-century success does not happen.

"And then," Tobias says, "once we've spent a little bit of time outside, depending on how cold it is, I might kind of cut that short and we'll come back upstairs and do a Q and A. Any question is fine. You can talk to us about our business model, the farmer-training program, or what's going on in the farm or expansion plans. We're a very transparent company. And it should be a really fun conversation."

At this point the lights dim and the video begins, narrated by Tobias:

"Before we talk about Square Roots, let's talk about the industrial food system. Right? It's a twelve-trillion-dollar global food system that is pretty much a disaster. Forty percent of food that is grown in the U.S. is wasted. A lot of food is actually overplanted by farmers outdoors. They have to kind of hedge against nature and, you know, they'll often overplant. And a ton of food is just rejected at their retail store because it just doesn't *look* perfect enough. Like, it is crazy when you start to dig into this system. Lots of waste."

He's absolutely right about all that. The global food system *is* a mess in many ways. According to 2018 estimates by the UN's Food and Agriculture Organization, over 800 million human beings go hungry, while around 2 billion of us are overweight and 600 million are obese. Bet nobody saw that coming. And the FAO figure for wasted food is pretty much in line with Tobias's—more than a billion tons of produce a year goes uneaten.

We need to understand that perfection in produce is an ideal, not a reality, and looks and taste don't go hand in hand. If we had grown that eggplant ourselves, we might feel differently. But today we're farther from the source of our food than ever before. The age of Instagram hasn't made us any more tolerant of produce that's as imperfect as we are.

Waste comes in many forms. The misshapen, bruised produce that's discarded on the farm, before we ever see it. The food that's damaged in transportation or storage. We know that about 20–30 percent of produce that makes it to the store winds up in the garbage—bananas turn brown before they're sold; lettuce wilts; tomatoes go mushy. Even when food gets to our homes, it isn't necessarily eaten. We see something in the store that looks fresh and beautiful and bright and instantly pick it up with good intentions to make something healthy. Then life gets in the way and that food sits around in the fridge until it no longer looks so bright or beautiful, at which point it goes into the trash. Or we buy six peaches when three would have been plenty. Two containers of strawberries because there's a special, though one was enough. I once heard my sister yell at her husband about his extremely picky produce selection method, "I want to eat them, not adopt them!"

Imagine the environmental impact we'll avoid if we can grow less and still feed everyone. There are several home-delivery services that specialize in fruits and vegetables that look weird and homely but are completely fresh and edible. Maybe at some point brick-and-mortar stores will try this too—create a section of ugly produce at bargain prices. Considering how many people of modest means already buy canned and packaged foods at dollar stores, this would be a natural if those retailers ever expand into fresh fruits and vegetables.

A few years ago, trying to do my part, I bought a composting barrel. It looks like an old-fashioned forty-gallon drum, only plastic. All our produce trimmings and table scraps go in, along with lawn-mower clippings, dead leaves, and fallen branches. The barrel fills up with worms and insects, which appeals greatly to the eight-year-old in me. Every few days the barrel gets turned, and those bugs give me clean black dirt, which goes right into our vegetable garden. In our house it's my wife who really loves gardening, which means that hungry worms and insects are her sworn enemies. But they remain my working buddies.

"You can also draw a direct line," Tobias says, "between the current food system that we have, which unfortunately gives us a lot of calories and not too many nutrients, and the obesity epidemic and diabetes and all these things. Not to mention it is an environmental catastrophe. Industrial food generates about thirty percent of greenhouse gases. And that's kind of ironic, really, because industrial ag is a driver of climate change, which is then putting agriculture at risk, right? And then one other thing that happens is because all the food that we eat is often shipped in from the other side of the world, we've got no idea who grew that food. There's no connection with the farmer anymore. And the sense of strengthening communities around food, which I think we all implicitly understand, just is not there with a lot of food that we eat today.

"Now, the good news is we're not the only people who think like this. Right? And especially younger generations, millennials and Gen Z, this is like their mission in life. The stats here are incredible. Twenty-two billion dollars' worth of food purchases have vanished from big food companies in the last five years. And they've all gone to local, smaller, independent food companies. This isn't just a Brooklyn-hipster-foodie thing anymore. This is a major megatrend that is having massive impact on big, huge, incumbent food companies."

Twenty-two billion dollars—that's a lot of money even for huge multinational behemoths to miss. Where exactly did all those food dollars go? Presumably, as Tobias reports, to not-so-mammoth concerns, since we're not eating any less than before—just the opposite. We all see evidence of the food revolution practically everywhere we look. Farmers markets and other nontraditional growing and selling. Online grocery buying, which puts small producers on the same theoretical footing as the giants. As long as I have an internet connection and a credit card, I can buy barbecue sauce from Texas or lobster tails from Maine or caviar from Russia or pasta from Sardinia, no matter where I live. Store brands like those at Costco, Trader Joe's, Sam's Club, Target, Loblaws, and many more have enjoyed great success at the expense of the old-school big brand names we once loved. Our awareness of how those major corporations—agricultural as well as manufacturing—have been harming our health and that of the planet. Organic gardening. The preference for local sourcing whenever possible. The growing interest in high-tech farming like we're seeing here tonight. The mere fact of food trendiness—Food Twitter! Food Instagram! Food Pinterest!—is proof that something is happening, a major shift in how we interact with the things we eat and drink.

"Another kind of indicator of this is the surge of interest and demand around organic foods," Tobias continues. "So, ten years ago, when I moved to the U.S., the organic-food market here was essentially zero. But that is now a fifty-billion-dollar industry. And again, that's all driven by people saying, 'We want food we can trust.' Right? 'I'll look at that organic label and I can trust that food.'"

Once again, back to that fundamental force at work in food today—the trust we once had in the food we ate; the trust we lost and now are trying so hard to get back.

"What's happening now, though, is people are realizing, okay, well, I can buy organic. I can buy an organic strawberry. But that's been shipped in from one thousand miles away and I really don't know whether it's organic or not. And so, I think a lot of people, especially in markets like New York, are beginning to see through organic. And you know, the next wave is local. And what people are saying is, 'If I know my farmer, I know the person that made this food, I can come to the farm and see it, then that's food that I can really trust.'"

He's getting at the balancing act that's at the center of enlightened food decisions today. The cost of one demand versus that of an opposing requirement. As Tobias asks, is organic but shipped from far away better for us, and for the planet, than nonorganic but grown a few miles from home? We've been informed by the experts about the health advantages of wild-caught fish and grass-fed, pastured meat. They're better for us, and for the environment, and are more humane to boot. So, we feel better about those choices, even though they're costlier. That is, until we're informed that our appetites are depleting the oceans of fish. And that there's no way the world's hunger for animal protein can be satisfied solely by grass-fed, pastured livestock, even if everyone could afford it—which they can't, meaning that our eating habits also collide with ugly issues of inequality and elitism. Nothing is simple today, especially not food.

In *A History of Everyday Things*, cultural historian Daniel Roche reports that the typical eighteenth-century French peasant ate completely seasonally and locally (of course), yet still managed to eat around sixty different things. We Americans today, with all the world of food within our grasp, consume only about half that number. Look at your own life as an eater. You probably have the usual things, like bananas, potatoes, onions, rice, chicken, beef, pork . . . but after the first fifteen items, it gets a little harder. So, if it's not money, or industrialization, or digital sophistication that determines the quality and diversity of our diets, what is it?

"And the demand for local food has increased four hundred percent in the last two years. It's the food industry's fastest-growing sector. So, again, it's not just a hipster foodie thing. This is a national megatrend.

"Now, there's a problem with local food, which is—especially local fresh food—it should come from farms near where people live. And increasingly, this is where people live—in cities. So, by 2050, our global population will have increased from seven billion to ten billion people. And seventy percent of those people will live in urban areas like New York. So, if you're looking at a world with an increasing population that is urbanizing very quickly, and yet at the same time people who want local food, then somehow you've got to figure out how to start growing food in the middle of cities.

"There are three aspects to Square Roots, which I'll talk about quickly. The first is the very scalable technology platform, which allows us to grow food indoors, in the middle of the city, and all year. The second bit is called Next Gen Farmer Training. This is where our farmers come from. And then, because we've got the technology and the farmers who are growing the food using our technology, we can run a really interesting business.

"Okay, so, on to our farm. You know, it doesn't really look like rolling hills and that sort of romantic notion of the farm, right? This is a very different system. But basically, what's happening inside each of the climate zones is we're replicating the best climate from anywhere around the world to grow certain crops. So, our farm is growing basil. Does anyone want to guess where the best basil in the world comes from?"

"Italy?" someone ventures.

"Yeah," says Tobias. "That Genovese basil is what everybody loves on their pizzas here. So, what we're able to do here is basically study the climate in Genoa. In peak basil-growing season, what is the temperature profile in daytime? And what is the CO_2 level? And what is the humidity level? And when does the sun come up and when does the sun go down? And we'll basically study all those parameters and then re-create that environment. So, it is always peak basil-growing season inside this container."

Theoretically, this sounds like a great concept. You could study the perfect growing environments for vegetables and fruits and herbs all over the world and then reproduce them anywhere you want. Italian tomatoes in Alaska? No problem. Japanese sweet potatoes in New Jersey? Nothing to it. Suddenly, shipping costs disappear.

But you still have to consider the labor involved, and all the technology. Probably not cheap, at least at the outset. And, at the risk of sounding crass, basil is basil. Good varieties can be grown pretty much anywhere, as long as there's sunlight. I had my first pesto at age thirty, and it instantly became one of my favorite foods. I still wonder how I could reach that age and never have been exposed. But the best pesto I've ever had wasn't made from basil grown in Genoa—it came from my garden.

The labor involved was pretty small, and all mine. It's true that, thanks to technology, our world is shrinking. There are modern-day Johnny Appleseeds everywhere. They do and try and dream up exciting things.

"And," says Tobias, "we work with young people on what we call our Next Gen Farmer Training Program. One of the areas that doesn't get as much coverage as it probably should is there is a demographic time bomb that is about to go off in farming. The average age of the American farmer is fifty-seven years old. So, who the hell is gonna grow all the food when those people retire in five or ten years' time? Right? It's a major problem.

"And the younger generations are not taking over those farms. They want to live in the city, which is where everybody else lives. And so, when we were setting up Square Roots, we sort of realized that we had an opportunity, really an obligation, to provide a pathway to bring young people into the agriculture industry. And we've got an opportunity to train them on some of these model systems. And help them launch careers in the food industry.

"And so that's what we do. Young people come in and join us for twelve months. It's a full-time paid job. We can surround these people with the hardware and the software and a team and training, get them up to speed really, really quickly so that they can become really good farmers in about six weeks. And then they take over running one of these climate zones. And then for twelve months they're our farmers.

"But in addition to that, in the background, they're also getting a really incredible education through exposure to every single bit of a local food system, from seed to shelf. And at the end of the program, many of the farmers end up joining Square Roots in full-time positions. But we're also equally happy helping people get jobs in other urban ag companies, or even setting up their own farms if they've really got that entrepreneurial bug already.

"Our philosophy is really the more of us working on this local food revolution, the better, right? And it's great if people want to keep working for us. But equally as good if they want to take the values and the mission and take that to other companies as well."

The farmer/grower of 2021 has very little in common with their counterpart of 1921. Historically, farming was passed on generation to generation. Today, the idea of going back to the land is for the idealistic and educated. All over the world, people with no agricultural backgrounds are being drawn into the world of growing and raising. I know a young film editor who started out with a little organic garden at home. His friends and family loved the vegetables and herbs he shared with them, and so he kept producing more and more, until he realized that he loved growing more than he loved film editing. At that point he took the plunge, rented a few suburban acres where a nursery once stood, and started a farm of his own. A few years later he has a couple of small fields he plants, three greenhouses that he operates year-round, and a whole lot of chickens that give his customers a steady supply of eggs. Everywhere, young people like him are doing similar things. Individually, their contribution to the global food supply is fairly small. Expensive too—it's not cheap to support your local farmer. (A dozen pastured eggs cost about double what the bad old kind runs you at the supermarket.) But these young idealists are changing what it means to be a farmer.

I've talked to small farmers with very modest parcels of land but great tech skills who make a decent living at it thanks to innovations like CSA—community-supported agriculture, where shoppers pay a flat fee in advance for produce they'll receive. It's a way of turning customers into investors and, even better, loyal fans.

"Okay, so we've got the tech and we've got the farmers. So, this is the food. In New York we sell our products through retail. And on the back of every single package there's a QR code that you can scan with your phone. And that will give you what we call the transparency timeline. That gives you a complete story of where your food came from, from seed to shelf. Literally, where did we source the seeds from? What day did we do that? Which farmer put them in the germination chamber? What did it look like in the farm yesterday when it was harvested? So, there is total transparency and also traceability in food.

"In fact, there was a huge scare with romaine lettuce a while ago. There was E. coli found on romaine lettuce just in the run-up to Thanksgiving. And in the U.S., they could not figure out where this lettuce came from. And in the end, they got every single supermarket in America to take *all* the romaine lettuce off the shelf because that was the safest thing to do. It was crazy because there's no traceability in the system.

"So, I was saying, in New York we distribute from our farm to over eighty retailers across Manhattan and Brooklyn. The really cool thing about this is that they're all within five miles of the farm. So, this isn't just local farming now; this is hyper-local farming. And that allows us to do some really creative things with distribution. There's no big eighteen-wheeler truck belching its way across the country and destroying the planet.

"And then, because we've got these kinds of nimble systems, we're able to get the food from farm to store within twenty-four hours of harvest. So, when you buy the product at the store, I mean literally that was growing in the farm yesterday."

It all sounds so great, doesn't it? But then I wonder, is the big bad food world really going to be meaningfully disrupted by shipping containers and grow lights and a young delivery dude on a bicycle? Can they really make a dent in a global food supply system that must feed several billion people?

"We believe this is a better system," Tobias says. "We're doing this in Brooklyn, which is good. That's nice, right? But we want to be doing this on a global scale. Earlier this year we announced a very exciting partnership with a company called Gordon Food Service. Two hundred distribution centers and retail stores all across the country. And what we're doing now with Gordon is building our indoor farms and running our farmer-training program on every single one of those distribution centers across the country. But I sort of think Brooklyn is like our pilot farm where we're figuring out how to do it.

"This is our mission as a company. We want to bring local, real food to people in cities all over the world, but do that by empowering this next generation of leaders, right? It's really important that we're not just building a company to generate profits, but we want to do it in a way that's good for the planet and good for people as well.

"Okay. So, with that we are going to head out to the farm. Here's the drill. We're going to go out through that blue door. I am going to be the first person out that blue door. Follow me out and I'll see you down there in two minutes."

And with that, we all head out, obediently trailing Tobias.

Now we're here—reunited in a parking lot, in the chilly dark, following Tobias to stand before what appears to be a standard-issue big, hulking, steel shipping container. And then he peels open the door and reveals an otherworldly sight. Picture a long, boxy corridor lined floor to ceiling with bright pink lights, a totally futuristic vision out of a sci-fi movie. Imagine *2001: A Space Odyssey* set in Brooklyn. In a parking lot. It's beautiful. Dazzling. Once your eyes get used to the cool pink glow, you can see the racks lining the walls containing . . . something.

Is this a farm? Why not?

"So, we've got ten of these boxes here. There's your twenty-acre farm. There's no soil in this farm at all. This is what's known as a hydroponic system. Our water source—we actually tap into that fire hydrant that's behind you, believe it or not. Obviously, it's purified. And then it's mixed with nutrients. And when you come up closer, you'll see there's an irrigation system in the roof of this thing. And the water and the nutrients run along the top and then drip down through the towers.

"The plants are held in these plugs, which are fully compostable. So, basically, the water comes down, the plant absorbs everything it needs in terms of water and nutrients. And then any runoff water is captured in a tray at the bottom and is then recirculated. You know, this farm will use about ninety percent less water than a comparable actual farm. In an actual farm the nutrients are in the soil. It rains. The nutrients dissolve. The plant absorbs some. But then the rest of it is just runoff. And it ends up in the ocean or wherever.

"Obviously, outdoors the plant is taking energy from the sun and converting that into biomass, right? But who knows what the sun is doing today? That means the plant will grow at a variable rate. Maybe it doesn't grow at all. It's very hard to run a predictable business that way. Indoors, you've got this extreme control where we understand exactly how many photons are hitting the plant. And so, we can really control production. And you'll see throughout the farm there are different spectrums of light. Basically, for different stages of the plant growth. And so, we can put exactly the spectrum of light that the plant needs into the farm. The whole idea is to grow as much food as possible using the fewest resources possible.

"Okay, so I'm going to stop and see if anyone's got any questions about the tech. Yes?"

There are the predictable very serious questions—you have to be a certain level of food nerd to be standing out in the cold staring at the insides of a growing container. People want to know about nutrients. Robots. LEDs. More detail than I can remember or would know what to do with. It's cold out here, so I'll spare us both and cut to where we all head back inside and upstairs.

"Okay. Who has got a question? . . . All right, so the question was around carbon footprint, right? And often when people talk about that, they'll want to know about what's the difference in carbon footprint between an industrial farm and an urban farmer. It's— And no one's got a great answer, honestly. It's more like, okay, what can we do to reduce our carbon footprint? So, for example, a new farm in Michigan, the company that we work with there, they, I think, on their energy grid sixty percent of their energy comes from wind. And then it's got to make sense to grow perishable food close to the consumer rather than grow it on an industrial farm and ship it in from thousands of miles away.

"And then the final thing I'll say on this, because it is a very— You could write a book on this stuff. My own home country, the United Kingdom, because of their intensive farming techniques that have been used there the last fifty years combined with climate change, the last projection I saw was that there are only fifty years' worth of harvest left in the UK. Fifty years. So, within some of our lifetimes, like, you will not be able to grow food there outdoors. And so, you can talk about carbon footprint all you like, but you've got to come up with a different solution quickly. Right? So that would be another way of trying to answer that question."

"What does that mean," someone asks, "there are fifty years left for harvest?"

"What it means," Tobias says, "is that by 2069 you cannot grow food outdoors in the UK."

"Why? Soil depletion?"

"Yeah, so basically the crops are growing out of topsoil, right? And that topsoil is eroding due to intensive farming techniques and climate change and the whole thing. And if that keeps going, there just won't be any come 2070, according to one study that I've read. I'm sure there's another study that will claim completely the opposite. But the point is there are enough, like, terrifying data points on the horizon to say, quick, we've got to go figure out alternative solutions here. Next question?"

"What other plants are you experimenting with?"

"Oh yeah, much more fun question. We're growing a range of herbs today. We have grown eggplants, tomatoes, strawberries, beetroots, Japanese turnips. We even had a chili-eating competition with some habaneros that one of the farmers grew. It was awesome. We've got cilantro and tomatillos going down there in the farm.

"The question isn't capability. It's economics. Basically, with photosynthesis, the plant is taking energy from the light source and converting that into biomass. And so, if you think about herbs and leafy greens, not too *much* biomass. Doesn't need that much energy. You can get that product to market at a very competitive price today. If you wanted to grow watermelon, you know, much *more* biomass. Much more energy. You wouldn't necessarily be able to get that product to market competitively today."

This is important. It brings us back to that delivery dude on a bike full of basil. The bigger the produce, the more energy required not just to grow it but to transport it and store it and display it too. I can grow mint in a window box. I can grow cherry tomatoes and zucchini in the tiny plot in my backyard. But, as Tobias says, try to scale that up and you see what agriculture is all about. It takes a lot of energy to feed an entire human being, let alone several billion of them, two or three times a day. Doing that indoors—to the extent to which it is currently possible—may cut down on environmental impact in some ways, but not all. Clearly, the future of high-tech farming will depend on solving some challenges, which is, after all, why the future (and technology) exists.

"So, we've been doing tomatillos, like little fruiting crops are probably next for us. Wouldn't surprise me if we got strawberries up and running here very soon. If you walk into the supermarket and buy one of every single vegetable and line them up from the lightest to the heaviest, that's like our product road map for the next ten years. Next?"

"How many farmers does it take to do ten containers out there?"

"So, right now we run on a kind of one-to-one ratio. So, one farmer, one box, roughly. However, that farmer is spending about twenty-five hours out of a forty-hour week farming. He'll spend about five hours a week on sales and marketing activities, getting out there and talking to customers, building the brand, learning how to get customer feedback. Five or six hours on programming, learning about plant science or entrepreneurship frameworks, whatever it is. And then four or five hours just kind of admin time and all that sharing time. But twenty-five hours a week of that is, like, *in* the farm, yeah.

"When we started the business, three years ago, the first thing that we had to solve was the farmer-training program. And so, the first year was really focused on that. After about a year we were like, okay, we can train these farmers, that's great, now how does this become a business? And so we started building our own tech platform. It's hardware and software.

"So, the hardware, as you saw, is one element of that. But there is a lot of magic in the software. There is monitoring the farms and providing instructions to the farmers and then learning what's going on and helping us improve the system. So, there was— In order to build this local food company at a global scale, we just knew we needed our own technology platform. And then, in terms of land, yeah, somewhere like Michigan— Actually, let me show you this because it's kind of cool. So, the really cool thing with the container then is . . . where do I have to— Steph, what do I have to hit to play this video? Is it 'N'? I can never remember."

He figures it out, and the video starts.

"So, the— This is kind of a beautified version of what you've just seen outside, with the ten containers. But what's lovely is you can pop up in a new market very, very quickly with these containers. Start selling food. Building the brand. And then as demand increases in that market, you can simply add containers and increase your growing capacity.

"And the obvious next question is could you stack the containers, right? And so instead of spreading out across that whole parking lot, could we just go up? These things are designed to stack seven containers high.

"And I'm not going to show you 'cause it's kind of secret, but there's a very interesting sketch of what one of our farms looks like that is not seven containers high but isn't just one container high either. So, I'll just leave it at that. All right, one final question then, from somebody who hasn't asked a question." And of course somebody does ask—a question about whether they can grow wheat here—and the answer goes on for a bit and winds up here:

"My sense is—if climate change is a catastrophe and we have to grow everything indoors, we'll figure it out, right? My sense is over the next twenty years or so, I would think that perishable produce will be grown this way, close to the consumer. And then things that will store and travel will still be grown on big farms. That's kind of the way I see it. We'll see."

And by this point, we're ready to shuffle on out of here, back to the street and the subway and home. On the ride, this is my thought: It's interesting and significant how this little high-tech outpost of future food coincides with the visions held by my friend Victor, formerly of Walmart. You wouldn't expect much overlap there, but I discover later that Victor and Tobias knew each other, and Victor is the one who's paying closer attention. "We need people who know how to leverage technology to grow food," he said. "The reason I love those guys is that they didn't start being the farmer, they started being the teachers, which is something I have to applaud. So, the entrepreneur of today will inevitably be part of the equation. Those entrepreneurs are laying the foundation of the tools we will use to feed the world in the future."

Will Tobias and those telegenic kids be an important part of the solution someday? Could be. Hope so.

EIGHT

The Supermarket of the Future

D id I say we were through with the supermarket? I misspoke.

If you study shopping for a living, there are certain advantages to working in an office full of normally functioning adults: everybody's an expert. We all spend our days measuring and analyzing how people behave in retail environments, and yet we are also those same people, out buying groceries just like everybody else. It brings a practical dimension to our scientific understanding. It also means that every time we enter a supermarket, we see it through a microscope, if you know what I mean. As a result, we all have strong, incisive views.

I convened a few of my coworkers one afternoon to discuss possible futures of the supermarket. When I read the transcript of our conversation, it felt as though I were reading a play—an odd play, to be sure, on a rather arcane subject, but a drama, or maybe a comedy, all the same. And so, I present, with no further introduction, the Envirosell Players in a production of:

A Long Day's Journey Into Aisle Four
A drama in one act

Dramatis personae

LARISSA, a suburban young mother with a baby and a toddler
DIANA, an older urban mother with twin teenagers
LIAM, a married, childless man in his thirties
PACO, a married man in his sixties

The scene: Four adults sitting around an office, all colleagues at a firm that researches how consumers behave in stores. As the curtain rises, a conversation is already in progress.

PACO

But how do you want the supermarket of the future to work? How would you imagine it into existence?

LARISSA

I imagine— No, no. Here's the thing. We don't *go* to the supermarket.

PACO

At all?

LARISSA

Very rarely. So, my imaginary supermarket of the future is me sitting at home. I don't even have to get up to check what's in the refrigerator. My refrigerator is telling me what we have in inventory and what we need.

PACO

Okay.

LARISSA

But I will need some way to—to get, like, my impulse buy, my sweet tooth, my . . . I want to try something new. I know all the things I *need*. I go to my basement, I see that I have plenty of Clorox—do I need it again? No, I don't. I can cancel the next shipment from Amazon. But I have to recognize that, or else they'll just keep sending it to me.

DIANA

Amazon doesn't know what you have going on at home.

LARISSA

Exactly.

LIAM

So, but do you now plan your indulgences?

LARISSA

I looked at my phone one time and up popped something on chocolate-covered pretzels, and—my mom had been getting us chocolate pretzels from Trader Joe's, so I said, "Ooh, that looks good." So I ordered them. And now it's become part of our regular rotation.

LIAM

I have a question for the parents in the room. I think we all, as kids, remember going to grocery stores with our parents as a fun thing,

125

a learning experience, maybe. But I want to ask just about how this works now and how you might see it happening in the future. Diana, you have older kids. Larissa, your kids are younger. As you start to split off some of your purchasing to online, and you do less in grocery stores, how do your kids ask for things? How do they discover things? How do they learn about things and contribute?

DIANA

First off, there's no kids going to the grocery store. There's no fifteen-, seventeen-year-old tagging along. They're done. So, in answer to how do they discover what they want—they get all kinds of influences. So, I'll text my kids and say: "I'm going to stop at the store on my way home, any requests?" And William will say: "Mochi." Okay. And, you know, it's these Japanese ice-cream balls.

PACO

How did they find out about mochi?

DIANA

Oh, well, at somebody's house, or they went out for lunch during school, right? Or there was a long phase where they wanted seaweed strip snacks; they couldn't get enough of them. And you're just sort of like, okay, what are you *talking* about? Send me a photo. So, you get it, but the pain in the ass about shopping for kids is just when you think you've found the magic formula—

LARISSA

Right.

DIANA

—that they like strawberry mochis, or sour cream, or cucumbers, or peaches, and you start making that part of your regular shopping list, they lose interest in it. And next thing you know, you have two cases of mochi in your freezer and nobody's touching it.

LIAM

But doesn't that happen to everybody?

DIANA

Right, but I'm not going to buy it if *I've* lost interest in it. But if I'm the primary shopper for three other people and I don't know that they've lost interest until I actually have bought it—haven't you seen me bring food into the office and put it on the counter? It's because it was rejected at home!

LIAM

Oh!

DIANA

Here's *another* thing. I bought these avocados two days before I opened them up to make myself some guacamole. Ended up throwing half—a whole one—away, basically, when you scoop out all the stuff you can't feasibly make into anything, right? So, food waste is such an issue because if you do shop only once or twice a week, you're trying to buy based on the ripeness of the food, the likelihood of when you'll actually eat it, and then if you're buying and cooking for other people, and your daughter may be in an avocado toast phase this week, and then—then next week she's not into it at all. But now, for instance, I'm getting lettuce that's grown near where I live in part because it's fresher and I know it's going to last longer.

LIAM

Wait, it's *grown* in Brooklyn?

DIANA

Yeah.

LIAM

Wow.

DIANA

Look, this is really my—*my* fantasy. I get off the subway, and as I walk out of the station, there is a thing where I can get all the food I want for that night in the amounts that I want, and all fresh.

PACO

Did you know that at bus stops in Brazil—

DIANA

I knew you were going to say some other country.

PACO

At the bus stops in Brazil, there are often these farmers markets where all the produce is pre-bagged. And so you can walk through, pick up the bags of whatever you want, and the price is written on the bag—two rials, three rials, whatever it is—so you can do your shopping literally, you know, almost without stopping.

LARISSA

I mean, that's why we have our meal-delivery service. That's—we use that for dinners for the adults, because it's something that we know we're going to eat and we know it's going to be healthy.

PACO

So, what everybody seems to be saying is the future of supermarkets would be no supermarkets. Right?

LARISSA

I will say that one thing that's stressful, that's come up with ordering online and delivery to your house, is that you cannot—you have no control over if they give you, you know, like a bunch of bananas that are really too ripe. So after one day they're inedible. You can write little notes with your order, but we've gotten a bag of mandarins that you could tell there was a moldy one in the center. It's like, they're not doing that thorough examination that you would do—

PACO

Oh, curating.

DIANA

I used online grocery delivery for a couple years when the kids were younger, and they would do things like, "Because you're such a valued customer, we gave you three extra grapefruit." And you're just like—no, because you wanted to unload some grapefruit, they're going to rot in my kitchen instead of yours?

LARISSA

Oh, God, no.

LIAM

Well, have you been to Whole Foods in the past little while? I go during the not-busy hours. Half the people in there, at least half, are store runners—the employees running around filling online orders.

LARISSA

Yeah.

LIAM

And they're moving at full speed, and it's not the same type of shopping that somebody who was actually buying the food would do. So, to your point, they don't give a shit if the avocados they pick out are as hard as hand grenades or as soft as mush. They just pick avocados.

LARISSA

Right.

LIAM

And they're not even the ones delivering it, but the guy who delivers the order drops it, and something breaks, and what are you going to do? Are you going to make a whole thing out of, you know, a dollar ninety-nine? No, right? For me, I would rather spend the half hour going to the store than the two minutes to write a shitty little note that's like: "You gave me the mushiest avocados."

PACO

Well, one of the things that we are looking at is the recognition that there are some things that give us some pleasure to shop for and others that don't. I like to go pick out my own oranges, or steaks, or loaves of French bread. But I don't enjoy my trip down the cereal aisle or the condiments aisle. And if once I've spent fifteen or twenty minutes buying the things that I enjoy, I'd love it if a store employee has pulled together everything else that I ordered and loaded it into the back of my SUV, and I've already been charged for it, too, so there's no holdup at the cashier. That would be great. I don't need to see my Thomas' English Muffins before I buy them. I don't need to curate that part of my food acquisition.

LIAM

How about this? Let's rebuild the supermarket so it's like a farmers market, where there's an outer circle of stands with fruit and vegetables, and the shoppers walk on the inside of the circle. And maybe the center aisle groceries—the pasta, the ketchup, the canned beans, the paper towels, the cat food—would be someplace else entirely.

DIANA

It looks like an Amazon warehouse from the outside.

LIAM

Yeah.

DIANA

But you go in through the pretty part.

LIAM

Uh-huh.

DIANA

With fake sun and fake rain.

LIAM

Exactly, and fake farmers.

DIANA

And fake farmers.

PACO

But the question remains—*are* you really buying all the exact same items from the center aisles, every week, every month, year in and out? I mean, there's always—there are new products where, like you say, the kids now hate brown rice and so you're getting Israeli couscous instead, or whatever, so in other words, it seems that . . . how would you ever discover anything new?

DIANA

Probably you would—I would say on every grocery shop, there's like five percent discovery.

PACO

But so how does that—where does all the innovation happen, then? If nobody's discovering new things, then there's no motivation for companies to innovate, is there? Because nobody will ever find their new products.

DIANA

I would miss that five percent if I didn't walk the aisles. Like I discovered sriracha-flavored pimento cheese spread. You know, you're like, huh. I'll try it.

LARISSA

I do sometimes even on the app, though, like I will look for— They have breakfast ideas, and I said, "Let me just see what's in there." I got Pop-Tarts the other day that—something I haven't gotten in years, but I was like, these are Whole Foods Pop-Tarts, so they must be good for you.

DIANA

Okay.

LARISSA

And they made me think of English muffins, something I hadn't had in years, and I was like, oh, I should get them too. We have breakfast sandwiches all the time and we've been doing brioche rolls, which we found on a grocery trip.

DIANA

Yeah.

LARISSA

And so there *is* some of that. I do a lot of impulse buying.

PACO

People say, "I'll buy this thing three times a year, and that's all." You won't buy it every . . . *definitely* won't buy it every week or every month, but three times a year, you'll have a crazy mood or—

LARISSA

Like I was saying about the chocolate pretzels.

PACO

Right.

LARISSA

Or like we'll make s'mores, but only during the summertime. It's like we have to have a constant s'mores setup.

PACO

Does it make sense for us to start thinking about sampling outside the grocery store, and that rather than getting you to buy the whole pack of something, if we can get you to try a sample we hand out on the street, that's a much more effective way to get you to try something new, rather than just sticking it on the shelf and hoping you see it?

LARISSA

Yes.

PACO

Or it could be a little stand at the farmers market that goes, you know, "Here, sample our new blah blah blah."

LIAM

But that's really more like advertising than retailing, right?

PACO

Well, yes, but I think it's also that combination of selling and marketing. Because there's a shift in consumption today from getting you to find the product to figuring a way for the product to find you. You know, Whole Foods' little kiosk at Kennedy Airport, which is feeding you a little of something now and selling you on the idea of buying it later. So the store exists in both places at once.

LIAM

Maybe. Because that's always been the main concern with everybody that we do research for—"nobody knows anything about our category." Our default advice is for them to educate the customer. But they can't do that with grocery staff, because they can't pay them enough.

But I *love* going to the farmers market. I go on Saturday—

DIANA

Okay, but are you also taking your kids to get haircuts? Are you taking them to—

LIAM

I can tell you exactly how many calories I burn on grocery shopping, and it's nothing.

DIANA

Do you have to carry the bags home? I used to use my own cart. And I would push that cart and annoy everybody in the narrow little aisles of our city supermarket. So, I'm like, I'm just going to carry this shit home. Only now the bags are hooked over all my fingers and my circulation's being cut off and I've got indent marks and my shoulders hurt, and I'm having to literally put my bags down on the sidewalk and just stand there for a minute to rest. That's just to get food home for my family.

LIAM

I know. But I'm just saying—perspective-wise—

DIANA

Now I just use the car.

LIAM

So, it's not that bad.

DIANA

Yes, it is. Now I have to find a parking spot.

LIAM

You're making shopping for food seem like it's the worst thing ever.

DIANA

Yes, it is. You wait until you have two kids.

LIAM

To walk a few blocks and choose the things that you and your family are going to eat later and—

DIANA

You've got it all figured out, haven't you?

PACO

See, Liam, for you, grocery shopping is labor-intensive in the same way that tennis is labor-intensive. In other words, it's an enjoyable activity. And so, the fact that it's labor-intensive isn't particularly a bad aspect of it.

LIAM

Yeah, I see a much smaller gap between the amount of time and effort it would take for me to figure out how much of everything I need and double-check that list and then set up a time to have it delivered and then the time spent worrying about how long it's sitting in there or the guy gave me a two-hour window and when is he going to show up so I can go on with the rest of my life. All of that, to me, is way, *way* more difficult than going to the grocery store and getting what I want. Like, time-wise, my way is faster, and effort-wise, it's easier. Stress-wise, your way is a loser. That's what I'm trying to say in terms of the alternatives.

DIANA

Yeah, and what I'm trying to tell you is, triple the amount of food you're buying.

LIAM

Yeah.

DIANA

When you're walking back home, triple the weight of the bags you're carrying.

LIAM

Sure.

DIANA

And double the time you spent in the store.

LARISSA

Yeah.

LIAM

Well, yeah, they have delivery—I would rather go to the store and say, "Hey, do you guys deliver?" and they say, "Yes, we deliver," and you do your shopping, but you don't have to schlep it home.

DIANA

Oh, so now it's a *little* less labor-intensive because—

LIAM

Well, yeah, if my problem was literally the weight of the bags, then my problem wasn't going to the grocery store or walking around the aisles.

DIANA

What would be *your* fantasy grocery shopping?

LIAM

I go to a place, there's no one there, and I can just walk through.

DIANA

Okay, so it's a grocery store as it currently exists.

LIAM

Yeah.

DIANA

But it's empty except for employees.

LIAM

I don't even want employees there. I'd rather—yeah, they don't have to be there.

PACO

He wants shopping online except he's in a physical space.

LIAM

Yeah. And open twenty-four hours. I can't sleep, go at two a.m., done. Yeah.

PACO

See, I mean, that's the appeal of all online shopping, isn't it?

DIANA

The downside to online shopping, though, is that there's no virtual replication of the aisle. So, a lot of the triggers that you have when you go through the actual store may never make it onto your list.

PACO

How about if there was? How about if it was like playing a video game? Where you have a joystick and you're traveling virtually through the whole store?

DIANA

Exactly.

PACO

So, then maybe video game designers should be designing online supermarkets?

LIAM

I agree, but does that mean you'd never go to that small specialty store that sells one item you really love?

DIANA

Well, I shop at one supermarket that actually fulfills *all* of my needs.

LIAM

Except that you still have the pain of shopping.

DIANA

Yes, but— To your point, if you go at a good time, then it's pretty nice. But I still have to park.

LIAM

And carry those bags.

DIANA

And when I'm in a store, it's on my time. Whereas when I'm at home, I'm everybody's bitch.

PACO

What are you saying?

DIANA

I literally have *one hour a day* where I'm my own person and that's about it, if I'm lucky.

LARISSA

Barely. I think it's ten minutes at this point.

DIANA

So, any way that I can have that hour I now spend in the

supermarket, and make it more of me not being everybody else's bitch, I would—

LIAM

So, wouldn't you dig, then, going to the grocery store for an hour?

DIANA

I—I *do* go!

LIAM

No, no, I know. But no one can bother you when you're grocery shopping. . . .

DIANA

And I'm telling you *my* pain points. It doesn't mean that I'm not going to do it. I can't say, "The hell with the groceries, you all can fend for yourself."

LIAM

I'm just trying to— I'm just trying to understand your— I don't mean to—

DIANA

I mean, can't we figure this out? Do I literally have to take my horse and chariot to town . . . it *hasn't* changed in—

LIAM

It has changed *drastically*. There are so many more options to—

DIANA

In *one hundred years*, it hasn't changed! You *still* have to go to a
location . . .

LIAM

Sure.

DIANA

. . . and bring your shit back.

LIAM

Yeah, but that is—that's *everything*. That's like saying, "I love
traveling, but, like, I hate carrying a suitcase."

DIANA

No, it's *not*. I mean, why do you think I have Amazon Prime? I don't
go to stores looking for HDMI cords anymore. RadioShack is *gone*.
Shopping now is click and deliver.

PACO

True.

DIANA

So, no, that's *not* everything. In fact, it's fewer and fewer and fewer
things. Fresh food is like the last thing that I'm actually going to go
and get.

LIAM

It's time.

LARISSA

What? To go to the store again?

LIAM

No, no, no. I mean, I'm reading this as more of a time thing.

LARISSA

Oh, it's time. It *is* time.

LIAM

Time's the pain point.

PACO

Can we back up here and go to that part of how your relationship to shopping and the different channels of shopping are governed by life stage? I mean, I *like* doing the grocery shopping that I do—I'm happy to be given the list; I'm happy to go to the farmers market. I get to talk to people—it is a social experience for me. But then, I'm not at the point where I'm trying to provide meals for a bunch of people on a daily basis. Is it that the grocery store of the future is going to be for single people and couples only? Is there a point at which I say, "Screw this shit, I'm going to order everything online, and when the kids go away to college maybe I'll go back to shopping in the store"?

DIANA

Couldn't there be some kind of drive-through— I can't get the shape out of my head, but where you get out of your car and it goes on a conveyor belt and gets loaded with all the staples you need while you walk along and examine fresh food and produce, and the meat, dairy, eggs, and fish, and when your car arrives at the end, it's filled with all the—

PACO

It's like a car wash!

DIANA

It's like a car wash. When you get your car back, it's been filled with all the groceries from the center aisles, while you've been shopping the stuff from the store's perimeter.

PACO

Right.

DIANA

And I meet up with my car at the end of the process, just like at the car wash, and I get in and go.

PACO

Brilliant.

LIAM

And your car would actually get washed, too, right?

DIANA

That would be awesome. And if you could pick up my dry cleaning, that would be good as well.

PACO

Why not?

DIANA

And my pharmacy order.

Curtain

—

We're not the only ones contemplating the way supermarkets will someday look and feel and function, of course. This is what all good businesses do, gaze into their crystal ball in an attempt to arrive at the future an hour or two before everyone else. In Italy, "The Supermarket of the Future" has existed for some time. It was the name of a project that the design firm Carlo Ratti Associati created, in 2015, for the Milan World Expo. The experimental store was part of a "future food district pavilion" sponsored by Coop Italia, the country's largest supermarket chain. It looked like a cross between an Apple store in Stockholm and the least cluttered, most elegant grocery you'll ever see. Of course, it held only six thousand items, whereas the average American supermarket holds around thirty thousand. The most striking design elements were giant mirrors hanging at an angle over the produce displays. When shoppers stood there, information about the fruits and vegetables appeared on the mirrors like magic, visible only to the customer.

The impetus behind the project was kind of unusual in the world of supermarket planning. I'll let Carlo Ratti tell you.

"In a novel by writer Italo Calvino," he said, "the protagonist, Mr. Palomar, walks into a Parisian *fromagerie* and becomes intrigued by the stories behind the food he sees around him. His observation is that: 'behind every cheese there is a pasture of a different green under a different sky.' This shop is a museum: Mr. Palomar, visiting it, feels as he does in the Louvre, behind every displayed object the presence of the civilization that has given it form and takes form from it.

145

"Calvino's short story was our inspiration," Ratti continued. "Every product has a story to tell—for instance, we can get to know where an apple was grown, or how much CO_2 was produced behind its cultivation."

Okay, a novel starting point, no pun intended. But he's 100 percent right: The idea of a narrative—that everything we eat has a rich backstory and we are determined to know it—is, as I've said already, one of the biggest forces pulling us into the future of food. Digital technology and social media are making it possible like never before.

"We wanted to use technology to re-create an old market," Ratti said. "After all, traditional markets were places for selling and purchasing but also arenas of interaction and exchange between people. Modern supermarkets, instead, prioritized function over social interaction, championing vertical shelving as an efficient method of dense product storage. I see the future supermarket becoming once again a space of social interaction and cultural exchange, also thanks to the new technologies. There is a possibility to create a peer-to-peer platform where information about the food products is exchanged in real time."

But there's also a force working against the impulse to know everything about everything we eat and drink: the time crunch. We all want to cut down on the time spent acquiring our food. Technology makes it possible for us to go grocery shopping in minutes, without moving, as long as we have a cell phone and a credit card. A lot of us will be happy never again to walk inside a supermarket.

"I believe that physical experiences will remain," Ratti said, "but we will see a bifurcation in the way we shop. On the one hand, we will increasingly use digital services (ideally, mobile apps) to purchase down-to-earth products—such as toilet paper, laundry soap, milk, and so on. Shout out to Alexa or Siri and they will constantly replenish your supply of toilet paper. This will happen from home, and it will be done as quickly as possible, perhaps just by saying a few words to Alexa or Siri.

"On the other hand," he went on, "I see a blossoming of 'experiential' shopping. Think about choosing fresh food produce: we will always enjoy going to a physical store where we can touch and smell. The store, in turn, can become increasingly focused on providing us with unique experiences. It is also what we tried to do with the Future Food District, imagining new experiences around products. In this case, people could spend more time if they want, but also could do shopping very quickly if they prefer so! In the digital era, the design of the physical supermarkets will be more vital than ever in crafting this sensory spectacle that Mr. Palomar found in the *fromagerie* in Paris."

I'm not convinced that Ratti's rarified vision of the future store will ever catch on, but one thing is undeniable: the space Ratti designed is beautiful, and I make sure to tell him so.

"Beauty will save the world, as Dostoevsky said," he replied, "and beauty is at the core of what we do."

And there you have it—a conversation about the future of the supermarket that begins with Calvino and ends with Dostoevsky. Just more evidence that when it comes to food, Italians really are different. But what will all this mean for the rest of the world?

The very idea of a "supermarket of the future" is intriguing to those of us who study shopping, but also to shoppers themselves. Maybe that's because we're all plain bored by the supermarket of the present, which is an awful lot like the supermarket of the past. When we opened an Envirosell office in Milan, we too were involved in an effort to reimagine supermarkets on behalf of a client, GS, the Italian retail giant. The concept was a break with tradition: instead of organizing the foods on display in the traditional way, we grouped them by how people consume them. So, for example, instead of coffee here and milk back there and breads over at the bakery, there was a "breakfast" section—*prima colazione*, I mean—with all those foods displayed together. Makes a certain kind of sense, right? And it gives us a new way to approach an old, tiresome chore.

The store opened with great fanfare and high hopes. It looked beautiful and innovative. But sales fell. You can sell furniture that way—lamps with chairs with rugs with window treatments. IKEA's signature move is selling entire rooms, not just individual pieces, in precisely that user-friendly way. Clothing stores assemble entire outfits, from hat to shoes, on a mannequin. But we don't buy groceries that way. Maybe you decide between cherries or grapes depending on how they look and what they cost. Broccoli or brussels sprouts? Watermelon or cantaloupe? Pork chops or chicken? Or perhaps your plan was to run in, grab the makings of a salad, and run out, and there next to the romaine you're face-to-face with steaks and French bread and Idaho potatoes. I think people are naturally suspicious of too much innovation where food is concerned.

Will the Italian reinvention of the supermarket lead us all into the future of food shopping? Time will tell. My question is this: When people consistently say they are pressed for time and want to spend less of it shopping for food, will they fall in love with stores that offer experiences instead of efficiencies? Or do we want both? Don't we always?

NINE

Shopping with Marion

We're huddled in a cramped little elevator, the size you usually find only in old European apartment buildings, on our way up one flight to a tiny Japanese grocery store, except we're not in Japan—we're in New York. It seems hard to believe that we'll find the future of eating and drinking here, yet that's where we're headed to meet with Marion Nestle.

It's hard to describe Marion's place in the world of food, because her role is both vast and singular and her perspective is unique. She's a scientist—a biologist. She is the Paulette Goddard Professor of Nutrition, Food Studies, and Public Health, Emerita, at New York University; she chaired the department from 1988 to 2003 and retired in September 2017, though for a retired person she still works pretty much all the time. She is also a visiting professor of nutritional sciences at Cornell.

She is the author of a tall pile of books, about nutrition (even pet nutrition), food safety, food choices, and especially food politics, a wide-ranging hot topic that provides the name for her popular website (www.foodpolitics.com). *Forbes* magazine once placed her at number two on a list of "The World's Most Powerful Foodies." She's the closest thing we have to a public ethicist on food and nutrition.

Her views aren't so rosy, as she has written:

Our food system—how we produce, process, distribute, and consume food—is broken, and badly. We know this because roughly a billion people in the world go hungry every day for lack of a reliable food supply while, perversely, about two billion are overweight and at increased risk for chronic diseases. All of us bear the consequences of atmospheric warming due, in part, to greenhouse gases released from industrial production of food animals.

But lest you get the wrong impression, she is a lively, funny, energetic eighty-four-year-old with many years of personal experience as a human being who eats and drinks, giving every pronouncement she makes a droll, down-to-earth, plainspoken edge. If I had a question about any aspect of eating or drinking, she'd be the first person I'd ask, which is why we're in this store. We're trying to stroll together, which is challenging in a place with very narrow aisles, especially if you're trying to have a conversation. And while Marion is small, I am tall. But we manage.

The shelves, of course, are filled with items exotic and mysterious, and labels that are untranslated. We end up doing a lot of guessing as we browse. This store probably couldn't survive solely on Japanese customers, but there are many esoteric eaters around here who flock to this place. There are no Japanese restaurant chains that rival Taco Bell or Domino's, but the food has an outsize influence in the United States. Once, sushi was exotic fare. Now, it's in supermarkets, often prepared on-site. You can buy it in convenience stores even, alongside the Big Gulps and the microwave pizzas.

We come upon something you'd expect to have prominent placement here—the tea aisle.

"Do you have more than one kind of tea in your home?" I ask Marion.

"Yes."

"Do you have *ten* types of tea in your home?"

"Probably. I like oolong."

"I am a ginger tea drinker," I say, "made from fresh ginger. I think ginger is one of the great secrets of the world."

"Have you ever had the Australian crystallized ginger?" she asks. "None of the others are any good. Just the Australian."

"I think my affinity for ginger started because on my grandfather's coffee table was always a silver box filled with candied ginger. Marion, besides ginger, do you have any other addictions?"

"Addictions?!" She sounds a little skeptical.

"Food addictions, I mean."

"I really like ice cream."

"Do you ever eat nondairy ice cream?"

"Not if I can avoid it."

We move along into the store's condiment aisle.

"Marion, how many different types of vinegar do you have in your home?"

"Three. At the moment."

"Do you have balsamic, cider, and you have—?"

"I've got wine vinegar, and then I have a white balsamic vinegar flavored with ginger. It is delicious."

"More ginger! I think you and I would get along just fine."

"But I can't have more because I don't have any room."

"Does that mean you have to throw out a vinegar to get another one?"

"Yeah, one has to go before another gets in."

There's something nostalgic about this kind of shopping excursion— browsing at leisure through the aisles of a small specialty store that manages to stock an amazing variety of well-curated foods. This old-school way of acquiring the things we eat and drink is on the verge of extinction—okay, maybe that's a little extreme, but it's definitely anachronistic and fading fast. Even before coronavirus, the shift to online was happening, thanks to the demographic forces I've discussed throughout this book.

But the growth of app-based grocery and prepared-food sales is not without its practical disadvantages and disappointments. I experience them myself, on a daily basis. "I am very frustrated living in an apartment in the city with food deliveries," I say. "A delivery person comes to my building and immediately rings all the buzzers so someone will buzz them in the door, and because I live on the first floor, just off the lobby, every delivery guy ends up ringing *my* bell and asking, 'Where is Two E?' The entire app-driven food-delivery system is predicated on a twenty-first-century technology that must operate in a nineteenth-century environment. And how many of us are even home all day to accept a delivery?"

"Sounds maddening," she says.

"Marion, do you ever eat that way?"

"Do I ever order in?"

"Using an app and ordering—"

"No, I don't have any apps on my phone. I use the telephone to call."

Even before COVID transformed how we eat, the new world of takeout food had become a flawed, impersonal process. On the rare occasions I order food to be delivered, I also rely on the old-school method of calling and speaking to a fellow human being. But the apps will win out in the end, I fear, if only because we boomer-phoners will die off like the dinosaurs.

"Well," I say, "I've made the point at my local police station that if somebody comes to the building and hits every buzzer because it's easier than figuring out which specific apartment he should buzz, then that's a form of harassment. Wouldn't you agree?"

"It would drive me crazy."

"What my situation says is that in our broader digital food world, the modern home is going to have to be built based on how people are actually living now."

"Which means daily Amazon deliveries."

"Exactly," I say. "But if we look at mainstream America, many families cannot accept a delivery at their suburban or exurban home during the day. They're not there. There are places where packages are safe left on a doorstep, but many where that just won't fly."

"Then that will be a problem," Marion says. "When I visited Barrow, Alaska, everybody got deliveries every day."

Increasingly, that's how the entire country shops. This is the great unsolved challenge of online shopping—we can order goods from every corner of the planet easily enough, but we can't figure out how to transport them the final ten yards of the journey. How do we get purchases from the delivery truck to our kitchens? Right now, it's possible to have deliveries left inside your car, which is then locked, assuming your car is home (and not in your garage) when you're not. Many people have their goods delivered to their workplaces, but that's now discouraged by employers, for the simple reason that there are too many personal deliveries clogging up our offices. It could easily double the delivery traffic at a small business and bring the place to a standstill.

So, the future home will be designed with a separate room—a space the size of a large closet, with an external door that can be opened only by an authorized delivery person. The driver will have the unlocking code, or we'll unlock it remotely from our phones when the driver texts us, and the goods will be left inside, safe and secure.

That fixes the problem for most people—those who live in houses.

We apartment dwellers still need a different solution. Could the twenty-first-century building have a cold room, like a refrigerated closet where fresh food can be parked? This will make even more sense in the post-COVID world. But it will create even greater distance between us and our food. No wonder so many of us struggle to re-establish the connection we once had to the source of our sustenance.

"Marion, you're a biologist, right?"

"I was," she says. "I describe myself as a lapsed molecular biologist."

"But you also got a master's in public health."

"Yes, in public health nutrition. This turned out to be a lot of fun, like falling in love. It was a very good thing to do."

"And did you know you would turn into what you are now?"

"No, of course not. I was going through a painful divorce at the time and just trying to survive. That's all. Public health school did just what it was supposed to. It opened doors. I was able to do fantastic things while I was there because the opportunities were so good. My summer fieldwork project sent me to Southeast Asia. I taught a course in Shanghai, did some consulting in Bangkok and Jakarta, met with a grant donor in Hong Kong, and visited Singapore—all at someone else's expense. I loved it."

"Was public health nutrition-oriented back then?"

"The Shanghai course was to teach high-level Chinese physicians and scientists how to flourish in U.S. medical and scientific institutions. In Thailand and Indonesia, I was sent by the U.S. Agency for International Development to find out what those countries were doing about urban malnutrition. The international public health students thought it was ridiculous to send me to do this, since I had never been to those countries and didn't speak their languages. I asked them, 'Should I not go?' They told me, 'Of course you should go, but don't expect to accomplish anything.' This was excellent preparation. When

I got to Jakarta, my AID contact welcomed me with, 'Oh no, not another American who doesn't know anything about Indonesia, doesn't speak Bahasa, and needs a translator, a driver, and a car.' As it turned out, I had been well prepared, did what I could, and found out what I needed to. When I reported in, I got an apology."

"But that's when public health and nutrition was about food scarcity."

"Right."

"Which is the opposite of today."

"True. That was in the mid-1980s, before obesity became the big problem."

We're still prowling the aisles. I'm searching for breakfast cereal.

"I didn't see it," Marion says.

"I don't think they eat breakfast cereal in Japan," says a young woman shopping the same aisle.

"No?" I ask.

"No," she says.

"I don't think so either," Marion says.

"It's not common there," the woman says.

"Paco, were you looking for Lucky Charms or something like that?" Marion asks.

"Nope," I say. "Doesn't exist. Not here."

"Now, this is a gorgeous package," Marion says, holding up . . . something. I can't tell what it is.

"Oh, it's tea bags!" she says.

"Can I buy it for you?" I offer.

"I don't want it," she says. "I just think it's a gorgeous package. I wonder what it tastes like."

Before we move on, I do what we're all supposed to do when we pick up an item we don't end up buying—I return the merchandise to the right spot. I try to be a good citizen-shopper, but not everyone feels the same shelf-responsibility.

"That's a big problem for groceries," I say as I finally find the tea's proper place. "People moving stuff around. You picked it up here and walked away, then realized over there that it's not what you want, but you put it back on the wrong shelf. The result is what they call a dirty store. And then inventory control—"

"—goes crazy," Marion says.

"Goes crazy. Because it's technically out of stock, but in reality, it hasn't been sold."

Even in a tiny store, shopping can wear me out.

"Marion," I say, "should we go have a cup of tea somewhere?"

"Sure," she says. "Should we invite that young woman from the cereal aisle? She was great."

I step away and see if I can track her down. I'm back in a second.

"Hey, Marion, guess who's joining us? This is Kristel."

"Hi, Kristel!"

"Hi, Marion!"

"Kristel," I say, "tell me, do you like this store?"

"Yeah, of course," she says. "I mean, I like coming here."

"What did you come to buy?"

"I didn't find my one thing," she says.

"What was your one thing?"

"Decaf roasted green tea. They have a whole bunch of the caffein-ated kind, but none of the decaf."

"Kristel runs a recruiting company for chefs," I tell Marion. "She does staffing for restaurants."

And with that, we adjourn back into the elevator, down to the street, and to the coffee shop on the corner.

"So, Kristel," I ask, "you must know a lot of chefs?"

"I know chefs," she says, "but I also know all the kitchen-stocking people."

"Where do you live?" Marion asks.

"In Hollywood. I've been coming to New York less and less, because I don't need to as much. So, it's like once every four months. It takes a lot out of me. And going to LA is so refreshing. Partially because I got sick of eating here—I live by eating according to the season, and it's so easy to do in LA, but back here I'm like, cabbage and apples and potatoes *again*?"

"Carrots," Marion says.

"Carrots. 'Oh, look, we have rutabaga. Yay!' So yeah, I'm a jerk. I'm one of those people who want to be completely seasonal and local but can't hack it everywhere."

"Ithaca has a rutabaga roll every year just before Christmas," Marion says. "It's a bowling contest at the farmers market. You bowl with rutabagas."

"When I was a kid," Kristel says, "we shopped only at the farmers market in Venice because it was cheap, not because it was a thing."

"And it's now a thing."

"The point is about being small, isn't it?" I ask. "Getting big is what ruins things?"

"Your goals change," Marion says.

"Right," says Kristel. "It's like if you're shopping for the best-quality food. If I'm shopping for just us, I'm going to buy the very best. But once I'm catering for three hundred people, I have to start making some exceptions, right? So, now I'm not going to get the top one percent; I'm going to get—"

"The top forty," says Marion.

"Or the top twenty percent. And it's up to people to decide, but they have no idea. So, it's actually on us to educate people."

"This is about class," Marion says. "Totally."

"Right!" says Kristel. "I'm now the one in my family who thinks I'm better than Costco fruits and vegetables, and it kills my mom when we go to the market and she wants to complain about how expensive things are and I want to complain about how worthless that packaged food is. And we're never going to agree, until there's, like, you know—I don't know *what* the solution is."

"The solution is governmental policies that promote healthy foods," Marion says.

"Yeah, that's why I was looking to you. I mean, we first need to admit that GMOs are bad, that we don't know what they do. We just need to admit that we're doing things for profit. We first need to admit that people are not allergic to gluten—"

"Let me just stop everything right there," I say. "GMOs have made a remarkable transformation in emerging markets as a way of feeding people. And we accept genetic engineering in so many other fields. Why aren't we willing to accept that a portion of our food supply is going to be GMO? It is a meaningful part of science, and—"

"I can answer that question," Marion says. "It's because Monsanto is such an awful company. Monsanto ruined it for everybody else."

Marion is referring to what makes Monsanto, the agrochemical giant, the personification of evil in the eyes of so many. It's somewhat complicated but has to do with the relationship between the company's pesticides, the genetically modified seeds it sells, and farmers who choose not to use its products. The problem with pesticides—insecticides and herbicides—is that while they kill bugs, they sometimes also kill the plants they're meant to protect. To get around that, Monsanto developed seeds that have been modified, at the genetic level, to be immune to its pesticides. A neat solution, in theory, but there's a big problem: once you spray that powerful killing chemical, it tends to blow beyond the borders of your farm and onto nearby fields and trees—killing plants and everything else in its path. And there's no way to prevent that, unless neighboring farmers also buy Monsanto's GM seeds, thereby granting the company a virtual monopoly—buy or die.

Add to that the fact that many European countries still won't permit GMO produce to be sold, due to fears of long-term health ramifications, and you can see why this is such a hot topic.

"Monsanto could have taken a very different approach," Marion says. "They could have been totally transparent, and it could have worked on problems in the developing world like it said it would. They could have tried not to destroy farmers. They could have been more honest about problems that they knew they were having. But they *didn't*. And that's the reality. I was at meetings of CEOs of major food—big agriculture—companies, and I watched them scream, literally scream, at the head of Monsanto at the time and say, 'You've *ruined* it for us! You've made it impossible for us. You have ruined our ability to have any public trust.' And that's what happened."

"Marion," I interject. "I was thinking about what five things every kid graduating from elementary school should know about what they eat, or just the five or ten things that *everybody* should know. Given your history as an educator, what would those things be?"

"Well, avoiding ultra-processed would be high on the list," she says.

"True."

"Which is sort of a new way of looking at it, and it's very helpful, and very well backed by research. Vegetables, variety . . ."

"Color?" I ask.

"Maybe for little kids, but I don't think about it that way. Vegetables. And calories count—you can't eat too much if you don't want to gain weight."

"But do you think a sixth-grader knows about calories?"

"Oh, absolutely not. No. *Adults* don't know about calories! You can't see or smell them; that's why there's this huge fight in the nutrition community now, mostly among physicians and journalists, not scientists, about whether a calorie is a calorie."

What she means is the debate over whether every calorie—no matter what kind of food it's from, healthy or junky—counts the same where our overall nutritional health is concerned. One hundred calories' worth of broccoli is no different from one hundred calories' worth of Skittles, at least where energy intake is concerned.

"Of course a calorie is a calorie!" Marion says. "But maybe 'portion size' is a better way to put it than 'calories.'"

"I think there's something to that . . . framing it in a way people can understand."

"If you want to know whether you're eating too much, you have to weigh yourself—it's the only way."

"I remember being a child of the fifties," I say, "when my mother would always say, 'Clean your plate.'"

"Right," Marion says. "But kids in the fifties weren't fat."

"It was a different plate."

"Very different," she says. "And it didn't involve snacking."

"That's right. Mothers weren't telling their children, 'Finish your Oreos.'"

"This was never a problem before ultra-processed food came along," Marion says. "That's the strength of the ultra-processed concept. I don't like the term very much, but it explains why people can't stop eating."

"Well," I say, "the other day I went out and bought my first box of Cheerios in probably twenty years."

"What on earth for?"

"Well, my thinking—"

"Cheerios is processed food," Marion says.

"Yes, I know it's processed food," I say, "but in the structure of my own kitchen, I don't think I've ever . . . Marion, when you say 'ultra-processed food,' what exactly are you talking about?"

"The term has a very specific meaning," she says. "The concept was developed by Carlos Monteiro, a Brazilian scientist at the Center for Epidemiological Research in Nutrition and Health, at the University of São Paulo."

She's referring to the NOVA food classification system, a way for us to measure the degree to which things we eat have been altered from their natural state. It's an extremely important thing to know today, for reasons that never existed before food was turned into an industrial product much like any other. The system was developed in response to the very question that bedevils so many people all around the world: Is this thing I'm about to eat good food or bad food?

You could say that if you have to ask whether it's healthy or not, you probably already know the answer. But most of us need a little more information.

Partly, the confusion stems from the fact that not every form of food processing is unhealthy. To explain the distinction, let's take a look at how the NOVA classification system, which divides all foods into four categories, works:

NOVA Group 1 is made up of totally unprocessed or minimally processed foods. That means anything we eat in its natural state—whole fruits, vegetables, other plants (like seeds, nuts, or mushrooms), meat, fish, milk, eggs, and water. This group also includes those foods when they have been processed slightly, meaning cooked, pasteurized, trimmed, chopped, ground, and so on. But that's it.

NOVA Group 2 consists of culinary ingredients that are derived from group 1 foods and used to prepare what we eat. Like butter, or oil, or sugar, or salt—things we don't consume on their own but are combined with group 1 foods to make things edible and palatable to human tastes.

NOVA Group 3 foods are considered processed but still may be healthy. These are the things made using items from groups 1 and 2, like cheese, yogurt, hummus, kimchi, sauerkraut, cured meats, wine, beer, and certain baked goods, like old-fashioned bread. This group also includes canned fish, fruit in syrup, and so on. The processing methods used in group 3 are mostly traditional ones that have existed for centuries. Food in this group usually contains no more than two or three ingredients—and, again, *all* coming from groups 1 and 2.

NOVA Group 4 is the danger zone—the ultra-processed foods, the scary new world of food engineering. Junk food—a phrase, as some people have pointed out, that's a contradiction in terms, because if something is junk, how can it be called food? Group 4 is a long list that gets longer every day. Sodas and other drinks composed of artificial chemicals. Refined grain products like chips and pretzels and anything else salty and addictive that are loaded with weird additives. Anything containing the ingredients that have become bywords for unhealthy eating: high-fructose corn syrup, hydrogenated fats, oils derived from seeds or plants using industrial extraction methods, artificial sweeteners, artificial coloring or flavoring, stabilizers, thickeners, preservatives, emulsifiers—there are new culprits added every day, it seems. Bread once was the most wholesome staple in the world, the star of more than one Bible story. In its old-school state, it is made with flour, salt and water, maybe yeast, sometimes eggs, or some herbs, seeds, or fruit. Group 4 bread, however, contains a long list of ingredients, including substances more at home in a chemistry set than a kitchen. The wheat has been so stripped of nutrients that they have to be artificially added back in. You can pretty much use this rule of thumb: if you don't recognize every ingredient as being something you might buy in a grocery store, or find in your pantry, you're in NOVA Group 4.

Simple enough, right?

Now, if this classification system were universally known and understood, at least we'd all be aware when we were eating something lousy for our health. But it takes time for any such wisdom to spread. And the entire concept is swimming against the tide.

In a 2016 study, researchers found that nearly 58 percent of the calories Americans consume are from ultra-processed foods. More than half! From "foods" that didn't even exist a century ago. You can see why our bodies are having a hard time adjusting—we're not made to eat junk and remain healthy.

And in case you assume that eating habits in other countries are any better, I just read that residents of the United Kingdom get slightly more than half their calories from foods in group 4. And less than 30 percent of their food from group 1.

According to that study, the more prosperous countries from the continent's north had the worst diets:

- United Kingdom: 50.7 percent ultra-processed foods
- Germany: 46.2 percent
- Ireland: 45.9 percent
- Finland: 40.9 percent

Now look south:

- France: 14.2 percent ultra-processed
- Greece: 13.7 percent
- Italy: 13.4 percent
- Portugal: 10.2 percent

To some degree, those disparities are a result of stronger traditional food cultures in the healthier-eating nations. Face it, would you rather sit down to a nice home-cooked dinner in Greece or England? Italy or Ireland?

But even if the NOVA system becomes widely known, will our eating habits improve? Once we know which foods are healthy and which are not, we'll have important knowledge. But we're still free to either act on it or ignore it. And for many of us, apparently, the latter is the preferable option. And maybe that's why the deck is stacked against NOVA or any other well-intentioned scientific attempts to promote nutritional health. Same goes for the federal government's regular updates on nutrition. In the end, many people ignore the scientific wisdom, not because they don't believe it, but because they'd rather *not*. It's in their self-interest not to believe what they know is true.

And there's another reason behind resistance to the campaign against consuming ultra-processed foods—the profit motive. Major corporations would lose billions in sales if we really stopped eating junk, which is cheaper to produce than whole foods are to grow or raise. Junk requires no refrigeration and is shelf-stable a lot longer than the perishables we should be eating. That's another advantage to edible chemical concoctions—they never go bad.

Will anybody ever find a way to reconcile those two opposing desires—to eat ultra-processed foods but also to be healthy? Maybe there will be a new wave of ultra-healthy ultra-processed foods, if consumer demand forces the issue.

Or maybe not. I ask Marion.

"Group four is basically junk food," she says, "but precisely defined. And because there's now this definition, there have been loads and loads of observational studies looking at people who eat ultra-processed foods and how that raises their risk for chronic disease.

There's one study for cancer, and there's a study that's come out on mortality. The correlations are very strong. But then there's an experimental study, never mind the observational ones, done by Kevin Hall at National Institutes of Health, who took volunteers and put them in a metabolic ward, gave one group as much ultra-processed food as they wanted. Everybody else had the other kinds, the not-ultra-processed foods, and he showed that at the end of two weeks the people given the ultra-processed diet ate five hundred calories a day more and gained two pounds in two weeks. When the volunteers were eating the non-ultra-processed foods, they ate five hundred fewer calories a day than the first group ate, and lost weight. Then they flipped it around and showed that it worked the same way no matter which group ate which diet. Absolutely fabulous work. I mean, that answers *all* the questions. That answers *everything*. Of course—people will eat more if they eat this stuff. I was telling somebody about it, a very large man who eats a lot, and he said, 'If I eat a salad, I never overeat, but give me a Big Mac, I'll eat five of them.' Yeah! Right! Those foods are *formulated* to make people want to eat more. And they do a really good job of it."

It brings us back to the point Marion and Kristel made earlier—the inarguable truth that big businesses are directed toward a single goal, profit, and profit comes with growth. How else can industries grow except by selling more—in this case, more food? If we each cut five hundred calories from our daily consumption, do you have any idea what the economic ramifications might be? Disaster.

And so, in a very real sense, corporate food needs NOVA Group 4 if it's to enjoy higher revenues and bigger profits. There's no other way short of a population boom, which isn't happening, or a sudden willingness among all of us to spend a higher proportion of our income on food and drink. Equally unlikely.

"Do you think, though, that at some point there will be healthier ultra-processed foods?" I ask Marion.

"Only with great difficulty."

"Like Beyond Meat, and Impossible Burgers, and the other plant-based meat substitutes, which I guess are—"

"Yeah. This is a big problem for them. People who think that these foods are the solution to the problem of killing animals are their core customers. I guess that's okay—those people don't care about processed food; they just care about not killing animals. They care a *lot* about that, as do the developers of meat substitutes. But I think that from a health standpoint, there have been real questions raised about meat substitutes, for good reason. What *I* don't understand is this: I see nothing wrong with being a vegan, but then why do you need a meat substitute? Why not just eat vegetables? I just really don't get it. Although it has been explained to me endlessly."

"You don't get the distinction?"

"I don't understand the need. If you don't want to eat animals, fine. You want to be a vegan and eat no animals whatsoever, fine. But why do you need a substitute for the thing you don't want to eat? Why do you have to take soy and make it look like meat? Why do you need soy bacon? You don't want to eat meat? Then *don't*. It's been explained to me how badly vegans miss those choices. That makes no sense to me."

"Maybe there's something in our brains that responds to burned flesh," I say.

"We're at the top of the food chain. Big animals eat little animals; that's what happens."

"I have eaten plant-based burgers, and there's definitely the sensation of meat; that's what it is. That's the reason for eating it; it's purely a sensory thing. There's a pleasure center in your brain that it touches—"

"Well, they've tapped into something that people respond to."

"That's why beets are in some of these products," I say, "because then the burger 'bleeds' red when you bite into it."

"Yeah, I've eaten them too," she says. "They're not bad. I went to the fancy food show and went around to every artificial meat and artificial dairy exhibitor. I tasted them all. I thought they weren't bad. A little salty."

"Obviously, a lot of lab work went into them."

"Yeah. But pea protein? I don't think pea protein is a good idea. It's been very bad for dogs. Anyway, they'll work all that out."

"Right," I say. "I think food companies will find a way to make ultra-processed foods healthy, or something they can at least claim to be healthy."

"Except they *can't* call ultra-processed food healthy. Because by definition, it's *not*."

"Okay. . . ."

"They can tweak it, they can make it less ultra-processed, but then so what?"

"But isn't one reason for its popularity that it makes eating so much more convenient, because it takes all the preparation, and the cooking, and the thinking, and everything else out of eating, and so that's part of the appeal?"

"Fine," Marion says. "You want to eat like that? Fine. As a health nut, it raises issues. The evidence is pouring in from these studies every day. It's amazing."

This turns the conversation to one of the most entertaining things Marion does on a regular basis. Every Monday, on her website, she exposes recent nutritional research that's either shoddy, deceptive, or flawed in some other way. Often, the research was funded by a trade organization whose members have a vested interested in the outcome.

"Has that become more of a thing?" I ask.

"Oh yes. This coming Monday, I'll post something about blueber- ries. There was just this awful study, really badly done, on blueberries, and there's also a journal supplement on blueberries, that the blueberry trade association is paying for. They must think it's the only way they can sell blueberries."

"Or sell more of them, I guess. I mean, for blueberries and avocados I guess the argument is, 'Well, it can't hurt anybody.'"

"That's one argument," Marion says. "I love blueberries, but I think this hurts science."

"But do you think that we'll get to the point where there will be fewer creepy studies commissioned to suggest that unhealthy foods aren't really so bad for us?" I ask.

"Well," she says, "the not-so-healthy studies are now more difficult to commission. Coca-Cola did it, and they got caught. Their studies fell into three categories. First, they said any evidence that shows that Coca-Cola is bad for your health is so badly flawed you can ignore it. Second was that sugar itself doesn't cause any problems for health. And third, they claimed exercise is more important for preventing obesity than what you eat. Those are the three big areas they funded, and they did a really good job of it."

"Right," I say, "until they got caught. Are there new ways these food companies have of lying that you're just starting to see now on the horizon?"

"I post practically every egregious example I can find. I don't post them all, but there's always something, some more outrageous than others. The sugar producers' association funded research to show that if you put sugar on vegetables, kids will eat more of them."

"I saw that!" I say.

"I can't make this stuff up!"

TEN

Drinking in America

W e've been out drinking. For a long time.

The bar currently thought to be the oldest on the planet is Luain's Inn, which opened eleven hundred or so years ago on the west bank of the River Shannon, in the Irish town of Athlone. That's pretty old, except I'm sure there must have been taverns for as long as there has been booze to imbibe, which means going back at least to China in the Stone Age, the year 9,000 BCE, where wine residue was found in stoneware cups. Roughly eleven thousand years of hanging out in saloons! We must like it.

Three of us have also been out drinking, though not for very long. But it's been instructive all the same.

The original plan was to meet two of my retail researcher colleagues, Clelia and Adam, at a cool-seeming place that had just opened: a museum/gallery space for art photography that's also a bar. With food too, of course. Fancy on both counts, no doubt, and with all the airs of a place that's destined for hotness—arty posters and postcards having announced its arrival, and website and social media all up and running months before the opening.

(This was pre-COVID, I probably don't need to mention. During COVID, drinking in public was greatly reduced, though more than replaced by the drinking we did at home. Liquor stores didn't suffer in the crisis, let's put it that way.)

Of course, when we called the place, we found out we needed a reservation, which could be made only on an app, and the only time we could get in on such short notice would be at 10:00 p.m. That's a little late for me to start drinking, unless I want to doze off into my dirty martini. And naturally, you had to pay to enter the museum if you wanted to drink there, which is just a cover charge under a different name.

So, we find ourselves instead at a drinking establishment maybe not as chic or exclusive but just as twenty-first-century—Starbucks. You've heard of it?

In America today, is there any commercial establishment as friendly and familiar, as warm and inviting, as eager for us to enter, as Starbucks? I'm hard-pressed to think of a massive corporate food and beverage provider that does the job so well. For years now, people on the sidelines of the adult-beverage business have been saying, "There is a public out there that is not being served well by the current drinks industry." What they mean is that we need more places where women feel welcomed and safe from the treatment they sometimes suffer at pickup joints or sports bars. Maybe Starbucks is one solution.

As you might imagine, the louche air of a real old-school cocktail lounge is somewhat missing from a Starbucks bar. It's not the kind of joint where you'll find Humphrey Bogart in a dinner jacket, puffing on an unfiltered cigarette. It's not even Cheers, since it doesn't feel like the sort of place where anybody will ever know your name.

The main floor of this gargantuan location is where the usual fare of Starbucks—coffee, snacks, free Wi-Fi—is served. The barroom is in a loft, slightly hidden, to the left and up a few steps, which is where we immediately head. The view from up here depends on which side of your table you choose—you could be facing the long, sleek, dark wooden bar, over which hang amber-colored glass globes, giving everyone gorgeous skin (which of course is the point, especially of restaurant and bar lighting, because—sex appeal). Seated along the counter are some young and attractive men and women holding elegant glassware containing colorful beverages. A swell-looking scene.

"Okay," Clelia says, "so as long as we look in this direction, we're definitely in a bar or a cocktail lounge. But you can still smell coffee up here. . . ."

"It's making your senses go a little crazy," Adam says.

Clelia and Adam have wisely chosen the seats facing the bar itself. I've ended up on the opposite side of the table, gazing over a railing and down at the ground floor, a scene that's unmistakably Starbucks—a place to go for your Salted Caramel Mocha Coffee Frappuccino, or your Pumpkin Cream Cold Brew, or just to use the reliably clean bathroom. Which is a definite factor here, since we're in a part of town where tourists tend to go, and where tourists go, tourists go. Downstairs also features a cozy fireplace, a working bakery that turns out muffins and croissants and so on, and a souvenir shop for the folks back home. From overhead comes the rattle of coffee beans being transported in pneumatic tubes to the roaster. All overhung with the perfume of coffee, as Clelia and Adam have already noted. A highly sensory experience.

Is it really such a surprise that you can sit around and drink booze at a Starbucks? Where *can't* you buy a drink today? The list has grown since olden days and continues to expand; it parallels the way coffee availability has exploded. Kind of interesting that alcohol flows so freely today compared to years ago, given our heightened awareness of alcoholism and the dangers of drunk driving. But the truth is that we're drinking more than ever. In bookstores. Museums. Movie theaters. Supermarket craft beer bars. Farmers markets. Near my office, pre-COVID, there was a Brooks Brothers (pre-bankruptcy) where you could go for a happy-hour glass of wine. In fact, when the inside seating area of this Starbucks was closed due to lockdown, it was still possible to enjoy a shot of bourbon—either in your cold-brew coffee or straight up—from a tiny bar they set up out in the street.

This place is Starbucks saying, "We can sell you coffee starting at 5:00 a.m., but by 3 or 4 in the afternoon the stimulant business starts to fade out. Still, we're paying rent twenty-four hours a day. So, is there any reason we can't take advantage of the fact that people like coming here, and they like our free Wi-Fi, and stay busy until midnight? We're already selling beverages to adults. Why not booze?"

"It feels like we've crossed a line when you can get smashed at a Starbucks, doesn't it?" I say.

"They served food and drink in the baths in ancient Rome," Clelia points out.

"They do at Russian baths now too," Adam says. "I was just there on Monday."

"Is there a menu?"

"Yeah, a menu. In a Korean spa, it's Korean food; in the Russian spa, it's Russian food and some Polish food."

Needless to say, the patrons are not solely Koreans or Russians. Given the adventurous ways of the millennial drinker, is it any surprise that even steam baths are now on the global culinary tour?

Our Starbucks-friendly waiter comes bearing drink menus. Most of the selections are variants on the usual martinis-cosmos-mojitos, and all include coffee. We each find something to try.

"Japanese whiskey right now is getting its fair market share,"

Adam says. "Taiwanese whiskey as well. Kavalan is starting to, and you know—"

"Hang on—what is Kavalan?" I ask.

"It's a Taiwanese distillery. They're famous for their single-malt whiskey."

"Okay."

"And a friend of mine who's a Scotch auctioneer is a good gauge for where liquors are being valued—"

"Your friend is a *what*?"

"I have a friend who's a Scotch auctioneer. He's a Swiss guy who's paid by a company to go to estate sales and know what's real and what's worthwhile and how to price it. When I go visit him in London, we drink several centuries' worth of Scotch in a night, all between one hundred and one hundred and fifty years old. It's mind-blowing. But when I go to Taiwan, for example, he wants me to bring back a bottle of Kavalan, which is blowing up because it's really good and they're using the heat of the Taiwanese jungle to get it ready to drink a little quicker."

"Fascinating."

"And the most undervalued liquor in the world today, as far as I know, is mezcal," Adam continues. "It doesn't have a good reputation, because of the border conditions and the way the U.S. market has treated it, and perhaps a bit of racism and classism as well. But right now I can get a bottle of top-tier mezcal for, at most, fifty dollars. You can't spend a lot of money on mezcal even if you try. If I bring my friend one of those bottles, he's going to sell it for seven hundred dollars, eight hundred dollars, easy, with people in Europe not really understanding the market or appreciating it fully."

"Wow, from fifty dollars to eight hundred dollars just by crossing the ocean."

"Yeah. So, what happens in the market, I think, is—as all these heirloom products from around the world become recognized, they go up in price. But then people start learning from them and replicating them domestically. When I was in Tokyo this summer, I was trying to learn more about sake, which is one of the big gray areas in my mind. I discovered *amazake*, which is an un-aged, unpasteurized fresh sake. And it's delicious, and I asked everywhere if I could buy it, if it was available for export, and I was told no."

"Why can't you?"

"Because it's not pasteurized."

Who knew what you can learn by drinking adventurously? We always think of globalism as a massive geopolitical/economic force, and it certainly is that. But it manifests itself in an infinite number of tiny ways, and food and drink have always been chief among them, going back to the ancient world of spice routes and silk roads. Our drinking lives exemplified globalism long before politicians and economists began throwing that word around. We drank wines from France and Italy, which opened our minds to those from Chile, Australia, Hungary, Portugal, Croatia. We learned beer from the Germans and the English, leading the way for brands from Holland, Thailand, India, Belgium, China. With our sushi we drank sake. With chicken in mole sauce, cerveza. We love them all, and in that way, we've happily become barroom internationalists.

Along with our drinks, our waiter has brought us little pizzas, a definite step up in free bar snacks from pretzels and peanuts. Suddenly, Starbucks doesn't seem like such a bad choice of cocktail lounge. We three have spent countless hours doing research for the adult-beverage industry, which has meant a lot of hanging around bars and restaurants and liquor stores and the beer aisles of supermarkets and convenience stores. If you can get hammered there, we've been there. And we've learned a few things about human nature.

Many drinkers walk into a bar or restaurant, or into a store, with their preferences already in mind—most of us have a certain amount of brand loyalty. We're all creatures of habit.

Can you guess which drinkers spend the shortest amount of time shopping in liquor stores? The guys (almost always guys) who drink Jack Daniel's. They don't even bother looking at anything else. That's good old-fashioned bullheaded boozing. Distillers love customers like that, but their numbers are dwindling. Middle-aged women spend the most time shopping, which is partly due to the fact that they're typically buying not just for themselves but for other people—dinner guests, parties, company.

The challenge for our clients, then, is to keep their own customers while stealing some from the competition. Curiosity drives change. That's how fads catch fire. You look around and see people drinking spiked seltzer, something you'd never even heard of. But it sounds good on a hot day. "It's today's special? A little cheaper than our usual drink?" Even more likely to try now. Ask the bartender, and she says they're tasty, and that seals the deal.

Or we're a fan of the Steelers, or the Dodgers, or the Blackhawks, or the Heat. And there on the menu card on our table, at the top of the cocktail list, is a concoction made in honor of our guys, in team colors, of course, as garish as possible, with lots of ingredients and flourishes and garnishes. A really huge drink, naturally, and high in calories, too, but who cares? We'll have one! Maybe two!

A good deal of what we know about how people drink is thanks to the Tobii system of eye tracking, which allows researchers to view the world from inside shoppers' eyeballs. Tobii consists of a pair of light-weight eyeglasses fitted with tiny cameras and reflectors. The cameras allow us to see exactly what you, the wearer, are seeing, both front and peripheral vision. The reflectors show us what your pupils are doing:

We can tell when your eyes are moving up and down or side to side, when they pause to glance or stop to look intently, and whether your pupils are constricting or expanding. We know when you're actually reading a sign or just browsing past it to focus on something else. In short, we know everything you see, for how long, in what order, and with what level of involvement. If you reach out to touch something, we see your hand same as you do. If you photograph an object with your phone, we see it on your screen. In a drugstore, we can tell whether you're reading the price tag on a bottle of cough medicine or the directions.

The view from the glasses is transmitted wirelessly, via Bluetooth, to a tablet, allowing us to sit in a corner and watch your brain work in real time. The video feed is recorded, naturally, so later our client can see too. We're all crowded inside your head, seeing the world through your eyes.

Like something out of science fiction. A little spooky, even to us.

In fact, if we wanted, the technology would also allow us to hear everything you say while you're wearing the glasses. But we never use that function, ever. Even our inquisitiveness has a code of ethics. Market research isn't Big Brother (yet).

When customers approach a bar, we've learned from Tobii, nearly everyone's gaze immediately stops at the same thing—the beer taps. Almost never fails. Once upon a time, there would be just a few—maybe two domestics and an import. Today, with the explosion of craft beer sophistication, you might find 50 or more on tap, and maybe another 150 brews in bottles. That tap section of the bar has become a traffic jam, with each beer trying to outshine the others for drinkers' attention.

People scan the taps the same way they read restaurant menu boards—from the middle out, meaning that the center taps get most attention. Brewers used to try to outdo one another by making their tap handles taller, but they went so far that now the short ones sometimes stand out most. Nobody really can read the words on the handles, especially while navigating through a crowd at the bar, so the ones with shapes or colors that pop—or with famous logos—do best.

Nationally, the biggest brands win this game, by sheer force of recognition (purchased with sheer force of marketing dollars). But there are plenty of regional stars, and their fans can pick their branding out of a crowd—there's a hard cider with an apple on the tap, a great example. Making attention-getting beer taps is an art, if you're doing it right.

A great deal of what we've learned from Tobii is thanks to Clelia, who usually handles these projects, in bars, restaurants, stores, and everywhere else. It takes a certain gift to convince people to wear funny eyeglasses in a public place even for just a little while. Clelia is sweet and friendly and lively, and more than 90 percent of the people she asks to take part say yes, which is kind of amazing in itself. She also speaks Spanish, which is one more advantage she brings to the game. But she's done this research all over the world, from here to China.

After her subjects finish wearing the glasses, Clelia interviews them to find out *why* they did what they did.

"I'll ask them, 'What exactly were you looking for in the vodka aisle there?' And they'll say things like, 'Oh, I was trying to find the one my sister likes.' Or there was somebody studying beer labels, and I asked, 'What caught your eye when you were reading two different six-packs?' And he said, 'I wanted to see which one had the most calories.'

"Or I'll ask, 'What were you trying to find in the prosecco aisle?' And she says, 'I was looking for a bottle to have with dinner with my mom. I was trying to find the prettiest bottle.'

" 'Did you?'

177

" 'No, I bought the one that was on sale!' "

"Clelia," I ask, "what goes on in the mind of a shopper as they walk into an adult-beverage establishment?"

"Well," she says, "I think it varies depending on space and time and purpose. What I see at a 7-Eleven in Chicago is very different from what I see at an Olive Garden in Columbus, Ohio, which is different from what I see in a bar in the East Village. And whether we're talking about males, females, twenties, thirties, boomers, millennials, whatever. But I guess it all comes down to purpose."

"Meaning that the process is different if they're going in with a girlfriend, if they're going with a tribe, if they're going with a boyfriend?"

"Yeah."

"Or if they're going in alone?"

"What is their purpose in being there?" she says. "Are they alone at the bar? Are they with the girlfriends, a girls' night out? Are they celebrating something? I think that's a huge factor in all this. Whether you're celebrating your breakup, or your promotion, or your father's turning sixty-five, or the fact that it's Friday . . . I think deep down, we see women and alcohol and celebration—and that's what I mean by purpose."

"Right. And they're not all identical."

"You know, I keep thinking back to one of the studies we did," Clelia says, turning to Adam. "Remember Moët?"

"Do I ever," he says.

"Moët came to us," Clelia says, "and they said, 'We just want you to go to Jersey. Go to the Buy Rite.' And I said, 'I know *exactly* where that Jersey Buy Rite is. And I know because that's *my* Buy Rite. I'm like, you're asking me to study *me*, basically. We really wanted to see what people were thinking as they shopped. What was in their minds beforehand, what were their intentions, what happened while they were in the store. And I was just shocked by the amount of sentiment and the amount of celebration and the amount just of *feelings*. I was just fascinated to hear males and females both talking about the sensations, the emotions that they get from a bottle—bringing someone a bottle of champagne, what it did to them before even getting to their event, what it did to them as they were buying it, what happened when they brought it.

"So, you bring a beautiful bottle of champagne to a celebration. And what happens? Someone opens it. And what's in that moment— it's the exhilaration of opening a bottle of champagne. It's the sound. It's the pop of the cork. It's the explosion of the bubbles; it's the feeling in your mouth; it's the sensations that you're going through."

Adam says, "And then someone's like, 'Oh, wait, that's not champagne; it's *prosecco*.'"

"Yeah!" Clelia says, laughing. "And you go, like, 'Oh, that was *prosecco*?' But it all comes down to purpose, to celebration and that hooray moment."

"Do you think people know the professional way of opening a bottle of champagne?" I ask.

"You mean sabering?" Adam says.

"No, I mean the idea that you don't just push the cork up till it goes flying out."

"As opposed to the boring way where you gently worry the cork out and get that sad little *pffft* sound?"

"Yes, you *worry* the cork out; that's the word."

"As opposed to blasting it."

"Right," Clelia says. "And not getting that *pop*."

"True," I said, "but also making sure that you don't spill out a quarter of the bottle."

Which, if you're only drinking prosecco, is no big deal, I guess, compared to when you're having real—real expensive—French champagne.

"You know, it was really fascinating to see them wearing the Tobii glasses and just going into the store and doing what they needed to do," Clelia says. "And even though the champagne-slash-prosecco section wasn't very big, it was big enough for them to browse one way, then the other way, leave, and then maybe go back for another look."

"And what did you see?"

"A majority of people *did* already know what they wanted. Or they knew because it's just what they always bought, or if they didn't know, sometimes they would ask for help. But when they were there in the store shopping, a lot depended on the bottling, the packaging, the gold foil. Who knew that putting some blue and silver ribbon on a bottle of prosecco would make it so popular? And it was just those things that really brought up a lot of emotions in people. Sometimes it wasn't the price point of the champagne or prosecco or sparkling wine that did it; it was the 'ooh,' the 'ahh,' the 'look how pretty it is.'

"I remember seeing a woman turning the bottle around and hearing her say, 'Look at this!' And I'm like, 'What are you showing me?' And she goes, 'This bottle is intended to look like a rose, but you wouldn't know that unless you flip it around to see the back.' And she tells me about how she found out that it was created by an intern for the company and it was kind of a design contest that this kid ended up winning. It's a pink bottle with a cute little rose on it. It probably tastes decent. But it was just those 'ooh-ahh' moments for them. And I mean, that's everywhere. I think when you associate alcohol, wine, women, males, anyone, it's that notion—it's the evoking of the emotions that matters most.

"So, for her there was a story. It wasn't just wine—it was wine with a narrative to share. That keeps coming up, over and over, when I talk to people about all aspects of food and drink. We want a story to go with whatever it is we're eating or drinking. Everything has a story to tell."

The reason we were hired for that study was because champagne producers are getting killed by much cheaper prosecco and domestic producers of bubbly wine who understand that it's all about packaging. And so, all these prestige brands that have had the same packaging for the past however many decades just can't compete. They haven't kept up.

Traditionally, champagne was purchased by men, for women—to spoil them, to impress them, to seduce them. We've all seen the movies where a bottle of the bubbly is ordered in some swanky restaurant, but have we ever seen a woman do the ordering? Male-female relations have changed a lot since those movies, you may have noticed. Women no longer need some stud to buy them fancy wine, just like they're not waiting around for him to give them nice jewelry.

Meanwhile, sneaking up on champagne's flank was prosecco—the much-loved (and reasonably priced) sparkling white from Northeast Italy. Once it caught on here, it opened the floodgates to sparkling whites and rosés from California and elsewhere.

"There are a few types of shoppers that we saw in that study," Adam says. "There are people who know the prestige brands and go to them. There are people who know the shitty brands and go to *them*. There are people who are playing the package comparison game. They're looking for presentation. And then there are people who *think* they want champagne but don't really know what it is and buy prosecco because it's a third of the price."

"Which is most people," Clelia says.

"Which is most people. Who just want it to mix it with orange juice and make mimosas anyway."

This is how brand names, luxury labels especially, have gotten muddled over the years. There are the shoppers who don't know a thing about a particular high-end category, like champagne, and they definitely aren't going to spend the big bucks. Then there are the knowledgeable, sophisticated shoppers who know a *lot* about champagne, or vintage Burgundies, or grappas, and don't need a brand name or an ad campaign to tell them what's good and what's better. That shopper isn't impressed by a name—they'll buy the lesser-known variety, the one only a connoisseur would appreciate. They'll spend big bucks on brands most people have never heard of. There's a cachet to that choice. And so, the big, famous label, the one that spent many millions of dollars building and marketing their brand, gets caught in the switches—*nobody* is buying it.

Well, not nobody, but you see what I'm saying.

"I think there's a perception that people who know a lot are snooty and only like nice things," I say. "And I think the way that we see it play out for customers in this kind of study is not true. It's generally the people who *don't* know a lot who default to these prestige names and labels. But the people who are actually a little bit savvy don't care about the name. Private-label products are scoring well in Consumer Reports studies; thus for many global consumers, private label is seen as a smart choice."

"So, yeah," says Clelia, "that was an awesomely interesting study."

"It was fascinating," says Adam.

"But then," Clelia says, "you've got the sports girl who just wants something to cool off at the end of her softball game. Which she's going to share with everyone on the team. So, is she going to change her mind when she's in the store because of a price point? Heck, why not? It's just for the team."

"But wait a second," I say. "Who's buying champagne for her softball team?"

"No, this wasn't champagne. It was in a 7-Eleven in Chicago, and the girl bought Miller High Life or something like that. Beer! It was a cute girl with a little bandana around her head and she's walking around in her huge athletic socks, and she's like, 'This is to drink after the game!' And I'm just like, 'Go for it, sister!'"

That ties into the single biggest shift in alcoholic-beverage patterns in recent years, perhaps the most significant change since the end of Prohibition: the growing presence of women in the drinking world.

Does anyone still remember the Ladies' Entrance? Youngsters, allow me to explain. Once, not so long ago, every eating or drinking establishment would have, off to the side of the main door, a discreet second entry, for women. The thinking being that no respectable woman should be forced to parade through the barroom itself, which would be crowded with men—probably smoking stogies, spitting into brass spittoons, throwing back heroic quantities of beer and booze (not wine—never wine), and possibly using colorful language. In short, a realm no decent woman should ever traverse.

Back then, it was actually forbidden in some cities for unaccompanied women to sit at bars, the thinking being that only a prostitute would dare park herself among so many men already indulging in risky behavior. The feminist firebrand lawyer Gloria Allred fought a Los Angeles city ordinance that barred unaccompanied women from saloons. And this was only in the 1970s—not so long ago. Even recently in New York, one fairly swanky restaurant still refused to allow women to sit at the bar, and it took a legislative act to force bartenders to serve pregnant women who wished to knock one back on occasion.

Ironically, women enjoyed more or less free access to drinking in public during Prohibition because then all drinking was illegal and speakeasies were beyond the reach of the law or guardians of public morals. It was only after the ban on alcohol was repealed that suddenly women were flagged. It wasn't until the sixties, when feminists demanded entrée into any place men could go—especially places like bars and private clubs where business was conducted—that the fight to drink anywhere women damn well pleased was rejoined.

Today, women of every profession can walk in the front door of a bar and sit and drink. That has had a transformative effect on the entire world of alcoholic beverages. (Although there are still plenty of bars with side entrances, vestiges of those weird old days.)

The biggest trends in alcohol today are being driven by females, mostly younger ones. Women, for the most part, don't drink to get shit-faced (at least once they're out of college they don't). They're playing beer pong, but they're not doing keg handstands. They don't want to puke on their own shoes or anyone else's.

The sports bar was created to be the man cave of public drinking, but there are many women who love watching games on TV in bars and love the convivial, boisterous atmosphere when passionate fandom and cheap buckets of cold beer come together. A sports bar on the night of the home team's big do-or-die game is a fantastic, thrilling experience. We've always played games in taverns, but it's gone way beyond darts and shuffleboard—now it's a beach volleyball court out back or an ax-throwing space for devotees of that peculiar saloon pastime. Personally, the combination of happy hour and hatchets makes me nervous, but maybe I need to get out more.

Brewers trying to increase sales always wondered why more women don't drink beer. The easy assumption was that they fear the calories. But there was more to it, we discovered.

We were hired to study how Brazilians buy beer and found some interesting mysteries. By our count, 70 percent of the shoppers inside their supermarkets were female and 30 percent male. But in the beer aisle, the numbers were reversed—seven men for every three women.

The women, however, bought more beer than the men. We were puzzled until we started interviewing shoppers and learned the simple reason: men bought just enough beer for themselves for the evening, or for the game they were planning to watch on TV. Women were the ones who shopped for social occasions—the barbecue that weekend, the family get-together, or just to have some in the fridge in case company stopped by.

But look at how beer is marketed and merchandised and you see that, for the most part, it's positioned as a drink for men. In Brazil, like the rest of the world, the beer sections of stores were decorated with posters of women in bikinis, or pictures of the St. Pauli Girl spilling out of her dirndl. It was as though the brewers were turning their backs on half of the population.

That didn't mean that the posters and other sales materials and ads should start showing good-looking guys in Speedos. We advised our client to depict groups of people in social settings—family celebrations, beach parties, like that. The way beer is actually consumed.

And then we realized that in order for beer to appeal to more women, another question had to be addressed: What had they been drinking instead? They must have been having something, and it was unlikely they would now add our client's beer on top of that. But our client's competition was wine and cocktails, we learned, the alcoholic beverages we typically associate with female drinkers. If women were to drink more beer, they'd have to drink less rosé wine, Aperol spritzes, mojitos.

Also, we were working in Brazil, where the warm climate was perfect for beer. If you're trying to quench a thirst, you can only enjoy so much rum or vodka before you're hammered. Whereas beer is perfect for sunny days.

When our client shifted their merchandising, the ratio of women to men in the beer aisle suddenly got much closer. More women shoppers now visited the aisle (and the men kept coming, same as before, even without the sexy posters). And sales went up too.

Brewers are waking up to the fact that if you have a better-looking label, you have in essence a different beer. You begin to attract a different drinker, maybe one who's willing to pay more for that bottle. Women may never drink as much beer as men, or in the same way. But we've seen that a woman is more likely to buy a case of the new IPA she discovered—rather than the same old Chardonnay—to serve with the salmon she'll be grilling this weekend.

———

Okay, we've had just about all the merriment we can have while drinking at Starbucks. But before we call it a night, I propose one last stop on our bar crawl, one that brings me back to the beginning of my education in American boozing.

So here we are, at an old-fashioned saloon with an odd name: the Ear Inn. But first allow me to back up for a moment.

My life in alcohol began as most do—illicitly and illegally. The first beer I bought for myself, back in prep school, was a twelve-pack of Ballantine ale, bitter and not to my liking. It was a reminder of my childhood, when my parents would give me a tiny glass of beer every Saturday morning. Hidden in that drink was the weekly dose of quinine I was required to take to protect me from malaria, which was widespread in tropical Indonesia, where we lived. Because beer is slightly bitter, it is a good way to disguise quinine, which is very bitter, and makes it tolerable (just barely) to a child.

Even in college, beer never became my thing. Instead, I would occasionally partake of Boone's Farm apple wine, a truly cheap and tasty drinking experience. But if you asked me at age twenty, my intoxicant of choice was marijuana. Hashish was even better.

Then, at the ripe old age of twenty-six, I found myself in the bar business thanks to a hasty and heedless investment in a run-down but venerable establishment in New York City. My partners and I didn't want to hassle with the red tape of getting a new sign approved by the city, so we covered over part of the "B" in the neon "BAR" sign, and the Ear Inn was christened. Today, SoHo is the city's ground zero of glamour, but back then there was nothing fashionable about our neighborhood.

Because I was now a bar owner, but a prudent one, my drinking life became practically nonexistent, and stayed that way for many years. If I drank three beers, I would get sick. If I drank two Irish whiskeys, I'd be clutching the bowl. My body just didn't tolerate it. Therefore, on the nights I tended bar, I was in a great position to observe drinkers and their relationship with the places they drank.

One of the first things that I realized was just how much of their disposable income our steady customers devoted to the barroom experience. I call it that because, clearly, it was about more than just imbibing alcoholic beverages. If that's all they wanted, they could have done it at home for a lot less money. Drinking was completely tied in with socializing. That beer in front of you gave you the right to sit in a private place of business, presumably a pleasant, hospitable environment, in the company of other social beings. Even the people who came in with a book or newspaper, or to watch a game on TV, chose to be surrounded by other people. There's no similar situation I can think of that provides such an opportunity. Not a restaurant, or even a coffee shop. It's part of what makes bars so special.

We did our best to make it a rewarding experience for our customers, something they could get only at our place. We were one of the first bars in New York to not only have draft Guinness stout, but also to serve it in genuine Guinness glasses we ordered from Ireland. We had some very savvy drinkers among our clientele, and they appreci-ated the skill required to properly pull a stout from the tap. There's a certain way to fill the glass and get the requisite head, and once our bartenders mastered the technique, our customers would sit there and drink all night until the keg was dry. I'd watch these men put away six or seven fresh pints each, one after the other, like a shared ritual. You couldn't do that at home.

Clelia, Adam, and I have been drinking for several hours now, long enough to justify ordering some food at last. The menu here is quite a bit fancier than it was back in the early days—it's a legit restaurant now, not just a dive with bar food. This trend has taken hold in most of my old hangouts, as everyone's culinary sophistication has become elevated over the years. The increased presence of women in here is largely responsible for that, along with the improved lighting and the higher standards of cleanliness in the bathrooms. I wish I had some final bit of wisdom to leave you with, but I've been up for too long and maybe enjoying the night a little too much to have anything useful left to say, so I won't even try.

ELEVEN

Brave New Eating

PACO: Tara, what are you having tonight?

TARA: I'm having chicken and steak hibachi with fried rice and vegetables from this new little spot. It's really good.

PACO: Paige, how about you?

PAIGE: Turkey burger with Brie, arugula, and cranberry.

PACO: Sounds good. I ordered a pizza.

I'm having dinner tonight with two women who were kind enough to try to educate me on the fascinating, strange (to me) world of Instagram food influencers—the people who post photos of things to eat and drink on social media, and the hundreds of millions of people all over the world who follow them.

I am at home in New York, eating at my desk. Paige Faustini, twenty-four, who has 124,000 followers for her account, @hungry hungry, is at her home in New York. Tara Bannon, twenty-five, who has 16,000 followers on @Charleston_Foodie, is in South Carolina. Google Meet brought us all together.

PACO: What kind of feedback do you get from being an Instagram food influencer? What do you hear from the people who follow you?

PAIGE: So, for the most part it's positive. I would say ninety-nine out of every one hundred comments are positive. Just like, "Wow, this looks so good," or, "Yum," or things like that. Rarely do I get anything really negative, especially about the food or restaurants. I think it's because I post authentically. I post all my own photos and my own experiences with food, so I feel like people look at it and think, like, *Okay, she actually went out and ate this and liked it enough to post it, so it must be good,* and they take my advice seriously. A lot of the contact that I have with my followers is just they're asking for recommendations, like: "Oh, it's my birthday this weekend; what are some good brunch places?"

PACO: What kinds of posts do they respond to?

PAIGE: Probably the biggest thing is Italian food. If you look at my page, the majority of the pictures are pizza, pasta, things like that. I do really try to incorporate a lot of different foods, because I don't want it to just be one thing. But there are certain pictures that I— Like, wow, this is one of my favorite photos I've ever taken. It's beautiful, the lighting is just right, and it'll get not so many likes. And then I'll take a picture of chicken fingers and French fries with my phone instead of my camera and it'll immediately get five thousand likes. I feel like the food you wouldn't expect—things that are not culinary genius food, just the basics like pizza, French fries, my followers love stuff like that.

PACO: Tara?

TARA: Yeah, I agree with that. I get a lot of tourists, people who will message me. You know: "I'm coming to Charleston with my girlfriends or my family or my boyfriend next month. What are the restaurants we can't miss?" Or: "Do you have an itinerary for us?" Or: "Where should we go? Where should we stay?" So, most of the people that I communicate with through my Instagram are people who aren't based in Charleston. Which is fun; I mean, I love that, because I love Charleston so much. I could talk about it for hours with any of these people. And I love sharing all my recommendations.

PACO: What are some specific things that people respond to?

TARA: If I feel like my engagement is down or I'm not really getting a lot of likes, I'll post something with an egg yolk. Yolk porn, people call it. So, if there's like a nice egg yolk breaking on a sandwich or a runny egg on a burger, those always for me do so well. And sandwiches. I'll go out to these restaurants and have these great eight-course dinners with amazing food, and it doesn't really resonate with people as much as me just like hanging off the side of a boat holding a sandwich. It's always the low-effort, no-energy ones that get the most response. Which I think just shows that people love authenticity. I think that comes through in those photos, and people respond to that more than these perfectly posed plates of food.

PACO: Is it really—is yolk porn really a thing?

TARA: Yeah, there's a big hashtag for it. It's huge.

PAIGE: Definitely.

PACO: Are there other things like that?

PAIGE: Cheese pulls are a big thing. Anything with a cheese pull, people go crazy.

PACO: Wait, anything with *what*?

TARA: That always does well.

PAIGE: A cheese pull. Like if you're holding up a piece of pizza and there's the melted cheese hanging down, or on a sandwich or something.

PACO: Huh.

PAIGE: Yeah, that's a big one.

TARA: I love cheese.

PAIGE: Going back to what Tara was saying, how if we post like a gorgeous eight-course meal versus just something quick and easy, I feel like the quick and easy things are more attractive to the audience because it's like oh, I might just want to grab a sandwich one day, and I would grab *this* sandwich. It's kind of like when they see a nice, well-put-together restaurant meal, it's like oh, but I would have to plan to go to that.

TARA: Definitely. Like they could just go and pick it up on their lunch break after they see me post it that morning.

PAIGE: Definitely.

PACO: What are the weirdest responses you get to things that you post?

PAIGE: I do involve myself on my page. I'll post pictures of myself with food, so sometimes I get weird responses from weird people. I feel very lucky to not have really experienced too much hate. I have had random people comment on things like: "This looks disgusting," or, "That's burnt," or something.

TARA: I get a surprising number of messages and comments not related to food at all. The first time I ever posted a photo of myself on Instagram, I received a few messages asking where my top and jeans were from. As someone who is so not into fashion, I was shocked people actually cared! Another question I receive a ton is people asking where I get my hair colored. After sending so many girls to my stylist, she actually gave me my own code, and now every girl I send over, we both get twenty-five dollars off!

PAIGE: The other night someone left a comment on a post where you could see me sitting at a table, wearing a leather jacket. She wrote: "Hi! So random but do you know where this jacket is from? I love it!" I answer those questions too. Sometimes my followers even recommend food or restaurants to me! They'll say something like: "Have you been to this restaurant yet? I went the other night and you would love it. . . ."

TARA: Back in May and early June, when Black Lives Matter was at the forefront of conversation, I went to this restaurant, one of my favorites in Charleston, and I started getting all these messages saying that they don't support BLM so I shouldn't be posting them on my page and I shouldn't even go there. And I had no idea one way or the other, but it was just interesting how people were taking that out on me—you know? And it's not that the restaurant said anything negative; they just didn't say anything at all when other restaurants were coming out with statements. I thought that was really interesting.

PAIGE: That *is* interesting. I posted a few things in May and June, when everything was really heating up, and I lost, just like that, a solid two thousand followers.

TARA: Wow, that's crazy.

PACO: You lost two thousand followers why?

PAIGE: Because I was posting things supporting the Black Lives Matter movement, and other things like that. I feel very fortunate to have this page with a ton of followers, but then when something important happens, I should be supporting the other things going on in the world too. And there were a few that I guess some people didn't want to see on a food page. They probably followed me to get away from all those things on social media. But you know, as the owner of the account, I have to make those decisions.

PACO: Who do you think was the first person to say, "The phone eats first"?*

PAIGE: I don't know. Looking back, it really felt like the whole foodie trend just happened overnight. Like all of a sudden, all these restaurants were making these crazy concoctions that at the end of the day almost don't even sound that good to eat. People just wanted to go and take pictures with it and try it because it was so cool and unique.

So, I feel like anywhere from five to eight years ago, things like that started happening. Black Tap in New York was one of the first places I remember. They had the CrazyShake with all these things coming out of it. And people would wait in line for that for three hours just to get a milk shake with a bunch of sugar in it. I think it's a generational thing, like people in my generation will literally spend all their money on going out to eat, going out to drink. They care about experiences, so they are really interested in that stuff. And they want to document it.

PACO: What's the breakdown of people who follow you?

TARA: Mine are mostly women who are probably between twenty and forty years old. I can look at the actual analytics, and Instagram shows you so much information. But for the most part, I think my account is like seventy percent women.

PAIGE: Yeah, I think my followers are like sixty percent women, forty percent men, and the biggest group is between eighteen and thirty-four.

PACO: In a normal week, how many times do you post something?

---

* It's an unwritten rule meaning you must photograph your food before you begin eating it. It was news to me.

PAIGE: I try to post at least once every day. I will say that in the past three months or so, I have been slacking a little because I did start a new job and I'm just not in the city as much, so I'm not actively getting new photos constantly. Before the pandemic, I would post anywhere from one to three times a day, and never miss a day.

PACO: Did you post today?

PAIGE: I did, yeah.

PACO: What did you post?

PAIGE: Yelp just came out with this big guide of New York City restaurants that are going to have heated outdoor seating. So, I went through their list, and I picked ten photos, ten restaurants from that list that I really like, and posted it on my page. Like: "Yelp just released this great guide, check it out, here are some of my favorites." And posts like that always get very high engagement, because again, the authentic part of it, "This food's not just pretty, I'm telling you that this restaurant's really good, I'm recommending it to you," it kind of gets people excited, that even though winter's coming you still can eat outside and enjoy food in the pandemic; I want to check this out and see where I want to eat. So that was a good one for today.

PACO: Tara, how often do you post?

TARA: I post probably once a week. Sometimes more than that and sometimes less. And some weeks, obviously, I eat out more than others, and I post more. And then other weeks, you know, if I visit my family up in New Jersey for a week, I won't post at all because I'm not in town. I mean, Paige's account is much, much larger than mine, and I feel like it's so much work to keep up with it. It almost feels like a second job. And sometimes I do get a little, like, burned out and I won't post for a few days. But Paige, I don't know how you keep up with it so much.

PAIGE: Definitely. I've had phases where I'll go a whole week without posting, but in the beginning, I just felt like posting every day was nonnegotiable, it was not an option to not check Instagram, not reply to people's comments. And now when I'm able to post, I will.

PACO: Tara, what's the last thing you posted?

TARA: So, if I'm not posting in my feed every day, I am putting stuff on my stories.* Like yesterday morning I went out to brunch with a girlfriend, and I didn't think any of the photos were good enough for their own post. But they were fine for my stories, and to keep people up-to-date with where I was going around town and grabbing brunch.

PACO: Have you ever posted a picture of quinoa?

TARA: I don't like quinoa, so I don't think I ever posted it. A little too healthy for me.

PACO: Paige?

PAIGE: Hmm . . . yeah, if I ever have, it would have been part of a bigger meal, like maybe with a salmon dish. But not so much. I'm more into the cheesy, unhealthy food too.

PACO: How much attention do you pay to the photography part of it?

TARA: I pay a ton of attention. I love a good photo. My friends will send me photos and they'll be like: "Oh, Tara, here, post this on your page. I had a great dinner last night." And I'm just like: "Hmm, I don't love that photo, but thank you." Definitely a little picky, I think.

---

* In case you're as clueless as I was: Instagram stories are casual photos or videos that appear briefly, then vanish; posts on one's feed remain visible forever.

PACO: I know photographing food can be tricky, and it can look disgusting if you don't get it right.

PAIGE: It definitely gets tricky. Even the most beautiful dish in the world, if you don't have the right lighting and the right setting, and you're just not capturing the angle in the right way, it just doesn't look good.

PACO: How do you shoot pizza?

PAIGE: Pizza is kind of an easy one because you can do just an overhead. And if it's on a plate, just like a triangle slice of pizza, usually pictures like that do really well. If it's a whole pie, it's always good to get like your regular shot of it, but then also one pulling a slice out. People *love* that. Pizza is definitely the fan favorite.

PACO: What's difficult to shoot?

PAIGE: I would say things like burgers are hard to shoot. If you just take a picture of it, all you see is the outside of it—mostly the bun. But then if you cut into it, you really have to style that the right way. I find burgers to be one of the hardest things to take photos of, and I love burgers . . . but it's definitely trickier than a plate of pasta or something.

PACO: Tara, what are your favorite things to shoot?

TARA: Definitely sandwiches. If you look at my account, you'd probably think all I eat is sandwiches. Because you open the sandwich and it just photographs so well. And you get to see each layer and every ingredient in the sandwich, and those photos always perform so well for me. And I also love to eat sandwiches. I mean, like a breakfast sandwich or a lunch sandwich. You can eat them any time of day! And the hardest thing I would say is when you're going out to a nice restaurant and the lighting is horrible and you want to get the photo, but you don't want to embarrass yourself or whoever you're with by using a flash. But then sometimes I'm just like, okay, it looks so good, I'm going to take the embarrassment and just do the flash really quick and get it over with. Everyone always understands that and thinks it's funny. But sometimes I just don't want to have a flash going off in a supernice restaurant.

PACO: Paige, you're nodding.

PAIGE: Oh yeah. I definitely have felt that way. I've learned to separate doing things for restaurants that invite me in because of Instagram and then just going out to dinner and enjoying myself without having to worry about pictures. Kind of like what Tara said, if I see something that looks incredible I'll take a quick picture of this because it looks too good not to. I try more to be aware. I don't even mind feeling embarrassed, but I hate feeling like I'm disturbing other people around me. Especially in a nice restaurant, and I have this big light I use, I feel like it's just so obnoxious.

PACO: Before dinner's over, one last question—in the final analysis, what do you think the appeal is of food influencers and social media and that whole world? Why do people love it so?

TARA: Before Instagram was even a thing, before social media, for like hundreds of years, food has been what brings people together and families together and friends together. Growing up, my parents were both great cooks and we all loved to eat and were always around the dinner table with extended family. And I think Instagram has taken that to another level, I can kind of connect with people in totally different states over our shared love of food, and we never even have to eat together in real life, but these photos kind of connect us. We build relationships based on our shared loved of food. It's the nice, positive side of social media. Now I live twelve hours away from my family, but being able to share what I'm eating on social media, they see that. Like my grandmother has an Instagram account just to follow *my* Instagram, and it keeps us connected, and she'll call me and say, "Oh my God, that thing you were eating the other night looked so amazing; how was it?" It's not as good as being there in person, but it keeps us so bonded and connected. Which is really nice.

———

Okay, so what do we make of this?

It's easy to be dismissive, in an old-fogey way, of obsessing over photographs of food that somebody else is eating. Especially because it seems to be predominantly a young-woman thing and we old fogeys have forever been scratching our heads over the obsessions of youth.

But I also think we're *all* slightly obsessed today with food and drink. We cast sneaky looks at what the person ahead of us in the supermarket checkout line is pulling out of their cart. We love rubbernecking at restaurants, trying to see what others are having. And think of all the news stories, websites, documentaries, books, and scientific literature devoted, in one way or another, to the subject of food. It's easy to say, "Who cares about what other people are eating?" But the answer is that many of us do. For whatever reason, we're on the lookout for what's new and what's next. We're being influenced. It wasn't always this way, I don't think, but it's this way now.

Of course, food itself doesn't really change much, except when we change it. Most often, that has to do with the ways in which we acquire and consume it—our habits. Our customs. Our foodways.

The revolution in those foodways is evident nearly everywhere we look. What we eat, when, where, how often, how much—all of it seems to be changing more profoundly, and more rapidly, than ever.

In some cases, it's change for the better. In many others, I think, it's for the worse.

Here's one major upheaval in our relationship with food that I find particularly disturbing. I read something not long ago describing a day in the life of a food app delivery person. It could have been about any of the companies, since they're all the same. The deliverers have to be clever and fast to make a buck, but even then it's not such a great job. The customers rarely even look at them—they open the door just wide enough to stick an arm out, grab their delivery, and disappear inside. (Since COVID, even that level of exposure seems too risky; the food is now left outside the door.) There's no practical need for human contact, especially since the payment and tip have been taken care of online. Imagine that, tipping someone you'll never see. I'm sure this gives cheapskates an easy out. I can't believe that post-COVID life will do anything to improve that scenario, which was social distancing before we ever heard the term.

Even having human beings deliver our meals might become a thing of the past someday, one more inefficiency squeezed out of the process by technology. I've seen tiny robots that are shaped like igloos and move at a walking pace, designed for making deliveries on college campuses. The charge is $1.99 and no tipping is required.

As a process, for all its inhumanity, app-driven delivery is really successful. It has completely transformed how some people eat. Not that they were necessarily cooking their own healthy meals before Grubhub and Uber Eats and the rest came along. They had the nearest pizzeria or Chinese restaurant on speed dial. But for anyone who came of age in the digital era, meals are just one more thing that we buy through the cold interface of an electronic device. I think there's something insidious and damaging about that. Without really noticing, we've become one step further removed from the source of our food. Now we don't even have to acknowledge the involvement of other human beings in the process of eating and drinking. I know people who acquire every meal this way, even breakfast. Can you imagine what your eggs and pancakes must taste like after a twenty-minute trip from a diner several blocks away? I'm betting this absurd practice doesn't stop people from complaining that their breakfast is cold.

And given the natural evolution of Web-based commerce, where every possible inefficiency is squeezed out, we have ghost kitchens selling food online—it's not even a restaurant, just an anonymous, industrial food-prep operation somewhere that's pumping out meals under a variety of trade names. I could start an Italian-Mexican-Thai-Greek meal delivery outfit tomorrow under six different aliases, and no customer would ever be aware. (Some wouldn't care either.) We don't even know where our food is coming from, or whom to praise or blame for it. Of course, this has made the whole category of online ordering ripe for fraud. There are crooks who operate under the same name as legit brick-and-mortar restaurants—they deliver food (and you can imagine of what quality and safety) using another business's name, while the real restaurant owner doesn't even know they've been hijacked. Until the horrendous reviews start showing up on Yelp.

Creepy!

———

Our cars would seem to be an unlikely force for nutritional transformation. Until you remember that we Americans have automotive DNA. We love our cars and do everything—*everything*—in them. So perhaps this should come as no surprise. Bruce Springsteen's anthem was "Born to Run," but "Born to Drive" would have been more accurate.

We've had drive-through restaurants since the 1950s, but cupholders only since the '80s, which raises a question: What did we do with our cups for three decades? We can only guess—did we hold them as we drove, or, more likely, did we manage to keep eating and drinking (even Cokes or milk shakes) and driving separate? When car designers caved in and introduced cupholders, they were the size of what would now seem like a very, *very* small beverage. Since then, cupholders have grown, to keep up with the bucket-sized drinks now popular in convenience stores and elsewhere. And where once there was but a single cupholder, on the front console, now there are many. I just read about an SUV that will offer eleven cupholders. Someday, maybe even that won't be enough. You can actually buy a minivan with a built-in vacuum, ostensibly to clean up Cheerios the kids spill in the back seat, though you know it will see some action around the driver's seat too.

With some exceptions, cars made for the European and Asian markets still don't do much with cupholders, in case you were wondering. Their traditional food customs have held the line against eating and drinking on the run—so far. But given the global adoption of American food habits, that could always change.

According to the National Safety Administration, more than 80 percent of us regularly eat and drink while driving. That's hazardous, of course. Studies have shown that eating while driving is at least as distracting as texting and perhaps as many as a third of all traffic accidents are caused by people who eat and drive.

Some of this habit can be blamed on the changing nature of work. Many of us are spending hours on the road, driving from one place to another, rather than working full-time from a fixed location. This means we're in cars instead of an office when hunger strikes. Easiest thing in the world—on American highways there are always plenty of fast-food restaurants to choose from.

The fact that our average caloric intake has increased over the years also plays a part—we eat more, and more frequently, than we used to.

And we enjoy eating in our cars, so why not make it easier?

In an article in the *New Yorker*, G. Clotaire Rapaille, a French cultural anthropologist who consults with automakers, said: "What was the key element of safety when you were a child? It was that your mother fed you, and there was warm liquid. That's why cup holders are absolutely crucial for safety. If there is a car that has no cup holder, it is not safe. If I can put my coffee there, if I can have my food, if everything is round, if it's soft, and if I'm high, then I feel safe."

Once upon a time, drive-in restaurants were a thing, where you could park, order from an actual human server, and eat without getting out of your car. A lot safer than our current habit, but more time-consuming, which is probably why those images of waiters on roller skates—carhops, as they were called—delivering your order right to your car window are now found only in nostalgia.

Given that we're going to eat and drink in our vehicles no matter what, it's surprising that carmakers have done so little to accommodate us. Aside from cupholders and vacuum cleaners, there's nothing to make eating any easier. No wonder we spill and drop so much on ourselves and all around our vehicles. What more could be done? Perhaps fast-food restaurants and car designers should collaborate. They could come up with an auto interior designed specifically to hold the packaging restaurants use for sandwiches, fries, drinks, maybe even foods that require a fork or a spoon. This could function in the same way airplane drop-down tabletops do, with indentations meant to hold plates, cups, and so on. At the very least we could use built-in napkin dispensers and trash cans. Our food culture practically guarantees that we're all going to eat and drink while we drive, so it's time that our cars caught up.

I wonder: Is a car microwave oven even possible?

Drive-through food has done its part to facilitate eating on the road. It's no surprise that burgers and tacos rule the fast-food menu, unlike pizza—a messier prospect if we're in motion. As a rule, car food occupies the least healthy end of the nutritional spectrum. By necessity, it's mostly sandwiches, fries, cookies, donuts; it would be harder to steer and manage a salmon fillet, or some nice steamed broccoli, or a stir-fry. So, here's another way that eating in cars has influenced our foodways—it's amplified our poor nutritional tendencies. Who knows how much healthier we'd eat if we never thought of cupholders?

On the other hand, car ashtrays and cigarette lighters have become nearly extinct. I guess that's a decent trade-off.

When you are a student of how people eat and drink today, you inevitably spend a lot of time thinking about the fast-food drive-through. In our line of work, you can devote decades to this: figuring the fastest way to get people through the routine of ordering, paying, and picking up; trying endless variations of signage and electronic ordering boards to cut even a few seconds from the process; observing all the possible permutations of where to locate the drive-through line relative to the restaurant and the roadway. That's a major issue, as you can imagine: if burger joint A always has a long line, you'll switch your allegiance to burger joint B, where there's no waiting—even if the line is shorter only because the food's worse. This is why drive-through designers try to position the window so the line of cars will not be visible from the road. By the time you see how long the wait will be, it's too late to bail out.

In every type of retail, from food trucks to banks to Versace boutiques, wait time is critical. Waiting is deadly. Everybody hates it. It actually distorts our sense of time—five minutes feel like fifteen when we're in a slow line. Our research shows that wait time comes in three forms: real or stopwatch time; perceived time; and some combination of the two. When businesses give us something to look at, or to think about, as we stand in line, then our perceived wait time—and frustration level—declines.

Having said that, I just read that the wait in the drive-through line at the first-ever In-N-Out Burger in Colorado was fourteen hours. So maybe under certain circumstances, we *will* wait forever if the food is good enough. During the peak of early COVID, when no restaurants' interiors were open, the line at my local Dunkin' Donuts drive-through was sometimes thirty cars long.

At some point, the drive-through ordering process will be totally replaced by apps, which are already widely used by people who patronize chain restaurants. You'll order and pay online, then just pick up at the store and zoom away. When that happens, a weird icon of American junk-food eating—the electronic fast-food order board—will begin its fade into history, and with it will go the experience of talking to a staticky, scratchy-voiced, disembodied worker who took our orders and then helpfully offered to supersize us.

Several years ago, we noticed something that no one expected. Restaurants assumed that customers who used the drive-through windows would either eat as they drove away or take their food elsewhere—to the office or home—and have it there. But that's not what happened, as we observed when we stood outside and watched. Many drivers would get their food, then immediately park in the restaurant's lot and eat there.

In hindsight, the appeal is obvious. Our cars have become our private dining rooms, like a second home. We can eat and read in peace. We can talk on the phone. We can listen to a podcast, or to music, or an audiobook. We can work while we eat, especially since most fast food is consumed with one hand, leaving the other one free to type, scroll, and click. Or we can just chill out. It's the best of both worlds—we're eating out, but alone and in a space we control.

Women, we saw, were even more likely than men to park and eat in their cars. Throughout the fast-food category, we've found, women—especially when they're alone—are more reluctant than men to eat inside. And when they do, they tend to choose tables that are secluded, away from the entrance and the main thoroughfare. Perfectly understandable, especially if they wish to be left alone by annoying guys so they can eat in peace.

And then we observed something really fascinating—that women eating in the parking lot drove more expensive cars than either the women *or* the men eating inside. Does some of that have to do with elitist nutritional shame at enjoying fast food? Entirely possible, for all genders. There's definitely a bit of status anxiety when it comes to patronizing the kind of restaurant that requires you to talk to an electronic menu board.

As a result of this habit, restaurant architects have had to rethink the relationship between the number of seats inside and the number of spots in the parking lot. Just one more way that cars dictate the terms of the food business.

Today, road food is everywhere. One of my colleagues just told me that the finest fried chicken to be found in the state of Georgia is sold at a gas station mini-mart. And when's the last time you saw a gas station *without* someplace to buy lots of things to eat and drink? Once, your choices were limited to Coke or Pepsi. Now you can assemble a full meal (of sketchy quality, perhaps) at any gas station in America.

Convenience stores originated as add-ons to gas stations. When you needed a late-night fill-up and a quart of milk for the kiddies at home, they were the ideal solution. As a segment of food retail, c-stores have exploded since those early days.

I love the whole c-store culture. It grew entirely in response to what drivers wanted, from the grassroots up rather than what some restaurant-chain marketing executives or private equity geniuses dreamed up. The stores grew organically into an important player in the eating and drinking lives of many shoppers—especially the ones behind the wheel.

Convenience stores harken back to the days when successive waves of immigrant groups dominated different retail categories. It sounds stereotypical, but like many stereotypes it rings true. Greeks went into the diner business. Italians had pizzerias or became barbers. Koreans opened dry cleaners and delis. Indian immigrants operated motels. For whatever reason, families from Iran and Pakistan found their way into convenience stores and gas stations. For people new to this country and our weird, distinctive ways, owning a c-store is a great education in American life, especially as it is lived in our cars. The path to membership in America is often paved with food. That's partly because you don't need formal education or fluent language skills to get started. It's also because all cultures express themselves through food. It's the common human language, just spoken in different dialects. And because everybody eats, everybody cooks, shops, or does both. We're all fluent in food.

C-stores are usually in high-traffic areas, but they differ depending on precisely what kind of road they're on. If it's a local highway, the customers are mostly people who live close by and stop in often to buy gas, or when they've run out of some staple—cigarettes, soda, beer, lotto tickets. You know that in a pinch you can get laundry detergent or cake frosting or ibuprofen, enough to hold you over until your next supermarket run. Local shoppers know their store's layout, so they're in and out, and don't require elaborate signage or assistance to help them find what they're looking for.

On main highways, stores get more first-time customers. It takes them longer to get their bearings and find what they came for. The transactions are slower. The signs in the store have to be bigger and clearer.

I talked to my friend Rob Easley about convenience store dining. He was an executive at QuickChek, a chain of over 150 convenience stores in New Jersey that emphasize fresh food—way beyond the usual salty and sweet snacks that stores once relied upon.

"Rob," I asked, "who eats in your stores?"

"When I look at my surveys," he said, "for the most part, I'm increasingly seeing that the younger generation, people now in high school or college, would rather go to a convenience store for their food. They're developing a negative view of quick-serve restaurants, like McDonald's and so on. At our stores they feel they have more choices—including healthy choices—and there's a perception that the food is fresher."

"And where do they eat it?"

"Well, the food that we sell, people mostly eat in their cars."

"While they drive, or are they staying in your parking lot and eating there?"

"Most of them eat it when the car's moving," he said. "There are small places to eat in our stores, but that's not the primary focus. Some are taking it home or taking it back to work, because they live or work within five or ten minutes of one of our stores. It's a combination. But most people are eating it, I believe, while driving down the highway."

Suddenly, autonomous cars no longer seem as dangerous as they once did.

———

In all the world of food, has there ever been anything more wholesome and life-affirming than a kitchen? Does any physical space promise sustenance, comfort, and companionship the way this room does? It's the traditional center of family life. It's warm in there. There's food and a place we can all sit facing each other. The kitchen table is like the symbol of harmonious family living. No matter how inviting the rest of the home may be, everyone seems to gravitate toward the kitchen and stay there—even when the cook of the house makes it clear that they're in the way.

There's also plenty of evidence that the more use the kitchen gets, the healthier we'll be. When we or someone who loves us prepares our food, we know there won't be any weird chemical additives, preservatives, or unhealthy junk in it. Loving hands feeding us properly in the home we all share—what could be better?

But this room ain't what it used to be.

"Is the Kitchen Dead?" was the title of a 2018 report from UBS, the investment bank. Maybe a little hyperbolic. But not entirely unrealistic. As a nation, we passed a significant landmark a few years ago: we now spend a majority of our food dollars on meals that were prepared outside the home. This includes dining out, ordering in, and prepared dishes we buy that require only a quick spin in the microwave. In 1930, Americans spent about 16 percent of food dollars that way. By the '60s, it was up to around one-third. Today, millennials—those born from the '90s into the early 2000s—are three times more likely than their parents to eat meals made by someone else.

Obviously, when you're young and without routine domestic responsibilities, you're more likely to eat this way. So, let's assume that millennials will modify their habits once they settle down—somewhat. But it's highly unlikely that they'll ever use their kitchens the way their parents or grandparents did.

No more kitchens! Houses built without them entirely? Or will the kitchen be just a fridge and a microwave for the meals someone else prepared? The end of cooking is not the same as the end of eating. Once self-driving cars are commonplace, nobody will need a license, but we'll still need a ride.

Because ordering in has become so effortless and costs have been driven down so low by competition and efficiencies, cooking no longer seems to make sense, especially to the young. Fixing dinner from scratch will become something like a hobby, like badminton or quilting. Or a thing to do on special occasions, like Thanksgiving. The fact that so many of us now live (and eat) alone—either in youth, in old age, or somewhere in between—only makes serious meal prep less likely to happen.

Of course, even if you only cook a few times a year, you'll still need a kitchen full of appliances, a twenty-first-century adult playpen. And you'll still need a flat surface around which you can all sit down and eat, on the nights when you give Netflix and the folding TV tables a rest. So, it's not as though kitchens will completely go away. We'll just use them differently. And while we may not make much use of a six-burner restaurant-quality Viking stove, or a Sub-Zero refrigerator-freezer the size of a compact car, that doesn't necessarily mean we won't buy them.

Kitchens in new homes are bigger than ever, but that's because they're now the main socializing room. Dining rooms are almost vestigial—who wants to waste space on something we use three times a year? Living rooms are nice, too, but it's been a long time since we did much living there.

There are a number of factors at work here, transforming how we use the kitchen. An important one, I believe, was rooted in a non-food-related technology: the birth control pill. Once women gained easy control over conception, they could spend years working outside the home, for as long as they liked. Without kids to tie them to the kitchen, dining out or ordering in suddenly was the smart, practical move. Whenever I go to a restaurant today, I'll always look around to measure the gender ratio. If the diners are mostly women, you can bet that the food and atmosphere will be very good. It's clear that women enjoy emancipation from mandatory cooking duties in a way that men don't experience.

This came about at roughly the same time as the decline of home economics as a subject to be taught in schools. Home ec was actually developed, back in the nineteenth century, as a way to increase the efficiency of women's domestic lives and free them from drudgery, not chain them to the kitchen. A young woman would go out into the world with that training plus a half-dozen recipes that her mother or grandmother had taught her to make. On such a foundation, future families were nourished.

In case you haven't noticed, not many young women are hanging around the kitchen with Grandma today, picking up tips. Even Grandma isn't hanging around the kitchen—she's at the office, or out playing tennis, then grabbing takeout on the way home.

But just as women were fleeing the kitchen, men were tentatively entering it. This was due in part to another non-food technology: how cars' innards changed. Once, a guy could express his inner grease monkey with his head under the hood of his vehicle, replacing spark plugs, changing filters and fan belts and fluids. When automobiles became computerized and accessible only to the pros, men had to shift their gadget lust elsewhere—like into the kitchen. Appliances that once were offered in tasteful pastels now came in stainless steel and chrome. Pots and pans got bigger and heavier. Knives became objects of fetish—large, lethal, hideously expensive. Grills were popular stove-top options, and where once there was Formica, now there is granite. We didn't need all those butch cooking-show chefs to tell us it was safe to enter the kitchen.

I had a "discussion" with my wife not long ago after we had guests over and one of them asked, "Who does the cooking in your house?" I said, "You know, when we have guests, my wife does it because she grew up in the restaurant business and it gives her joy to cook for eight people. But when it's just the two of us, I do a lot of the cooking."

After company left, my wife said, "You *used* to do a lot of the cooking, and now *I* do a lot of the just-you-and-me cooking."

To which I replied, "But if you look at the years we've been together, okay, and you look at the nights when it was just the two of us, sixty-five percent of those nights I produced the meals. But yes, in the past two years when you haven't— When I've been working and yes, you've been working, too, there has been some shift. But I'm still eminently more comfortable as the member of this couple who cooks for two of us than I am cooking for eight."

In case you missed it, my concession was tucked in there. In that exchange, I see how relations between significant others regarding the kitchen have evolved in recent years, at least around our house.

My relationship to cooking has changed a lot thanks to YouTube. I've always *hated* washing pots, but I found a video that showed me how to cook in the oven using parchment paper. The fish or meat or whatever goes inside the paper, and the whole thing goes into the oven, and when it's done, there's no cleanup. The paper only caught fire once, and I learned from that experience how to fold it properly, to prevent it from touching the heating element. An important lesson. My love affair with the oven started.

This taught me that maybe I wasn't completely helpless in the kitchen, and since then YouTube has been my excellent cooking tutor. Once upon a time, I might have opened a cookbook or two and tried to read and cook at the same time. Now, I can watch somebody prepare a dish—repeatedly, if necessary, and hitting pause as required—before

I try my hand. YouTube has become the global do-it-yourself coach, not just for wannabe chefs but for anybody attempting anything new.

My wife was recently sick with a fever and sore throat and all the rest.

"What can I do for you?" I asked, and she replied, "I want chicken soup, and I want you to make it with ginger and garlic and potatoes and you can put the broccoli in last, okay?"

I don't know if that's the answer I expected, but I was prepared, even though it was seven o'clock in the evening, meaning I had to move fast. If we had some store-bought chicken stock or broth lying around, I might have been tempted, but we didn't. So, I put a big pot of water on a low flame, and then I ran out to buy the chicken and other ingredients on her list. Once I got home, I started the chicken parts in a frying pan while I prepped the vegetables and threw them in the boiling water. And before too long, she had her chicken soup, made to her specifications (more or less). She felt better, and you know, I felt pretty good too.

I don't feel bashful saying this was probably the high point of my life as a chef—being able to marshal all those ingredients and deploy two pots at the same time, and for a great cause.

The only thing better than a nourishing, healthy two-pot meal is a one-pot meal, which is how many of us cook today. As a practical matter, the biggest star of the cutting-edge kitchen is not the steam oven or the smart refrigerator or the $200 ceramic carving knife, but the slow cooker, where you can assemble all the ingredients in the morning, get the meal going, leave for work, and come home eight or ten hours later to find dinner completely made, at the perfect temperature, ready to eat. Doesn't this sound like the way we would have cooked in the hearth a century or more ago? The engineer who designed the modern slow cooker was supposedly inspired by his grandmother, who told him of a stew that cooked all day back in her native Lithuania.

As I've written already, I grew up strangely, kitchen-wise—mostly in Asian countries where the staff prepared all our meals. The kitchen boss was always male, and his helpers generally were female. Yet Mr. Wong, our cook in Korea—whom I often watched as he worked—would go home and let his wife do all the cooking, while he sat, drank beer, and smoked cigarettes.

So, I grew up thinking that men belonged in the kitchen, though I was still without many culinary chops of my own. That lasted until I grew up and moved out and was far too poor to hire chefs or eat in restaurants. Today, having survived decades of unmarried life, I am handy enough in the kitchen. At one point, a few years ago, I even designed a customized stove: two burners at the usual height and the other two a little lower, to make it easier to fry in one pan while stirring another. Every cook and kitchen designer who has seen it loves it. I may have missed my calling.

We've done research for some of the world's largest home builders on what buyers want in kitchen technology. The target groups have mostly been young families considering town houses. One client's overall theme was "smarter living," which meant, first of all, homes where Wi-Fi connectivity was built in, not added on, and left no area uncovered. The way we all wish we had it.

In those houses, parents can check their video baby monitors no matter where they are—from the kitchen while cooking, or even on the way home from work. They can also preheat the oven remotely, and once they're in the kitchen and fixing dinner, they can make sure the kids are doing homework instead of playing video games. Needless to say, all this technology was a useful selling tool. The kitchen of tomorrow can be the hub of the home only if you can see and control everything while you're in there.

By now most people are familiar with the concept of the "smart" kitchen—one where the major appliances are all connected to the internet and keep track of what we have and what we need. We worked on a project called the Samsung Experience Center, a look at the kitchen of the future—where almost everything is connected. Right now, Alexa is but a baby step. Someday, you won't even need to remind her to order oat bran, since the pantry shelf will know that you're out of it and automatically make the addition to your digital shopping list.

The concept of a huge, wide-open, high-tech kitchen that can be used by everyone in the family, for practically any purpose, is a purely American thing so far. It fits in with our national DNA—it's casual, dynamic, up for anything.

My Japanese friends are deeply puzzled by the open kitchen. What bothers them most, I learned, is the fact that everyone can see the mess after a meal has been prepared. They'd rather spare their guests that view, and I can't say I disagree completely. But it's just not our way, spiritually speaking—we Americans prefer to let it *all* hang out. Of course, Japanese homes are usually smaller than ours, and so they must use space as efficiently as possible. In Japan, when you shop for a new refrigerator, often you'll bring photos of your kitchen and the inside of your current fridge, so the shelving in the new one can be custom designed to suit your particular needs. Which is a cool idea, I think—if you usually have lots of tall wine bottles in there, for instance, the shelves should be arranged differently than if you're a beer drinker or no drinker at all.

Our freewheeling foodways may be a harbinger of the future of eating and drinking. But it will take the rest of the world a little more time to catch up. My international visitors are always surprised—and slightly nauseated—to see how nonchalantly we Americans chow down while walking city streets. Foreigners are queasy at the sight of us eating on public transportation, or while strolling around town, or seated on a curb, especially when it's something challenging like an oily slice of pizza on a paper plate, or a burger, fries, and soda. I once brought some visiting Japanese guests on the subway, where a teenager was enjoying his takeout lunch with lots of fragrant onions. It was not a high point of their trip.

———

I don't know if you noticed, but there's a common denominator in this chapter so far: young people disrupting our treasured old foodways. Not surprising at all, I realize—young people have always been prime disruptors. It's their job. I can almost guarantee that every food-related impulse of theirs will only become more prevalent in the future, as those youths grow older and take over. As we've seen throughout this book, many of the positive movements in the world of food are thanks to idealistic young people. But there are also some weird ways that the young embrace.

I can see harbingers of this in my own home. Our kids' friends love coming for dinner. We set a table old-school, and we talk while we eat, with phones off. Our guests say that at their homes, many meals are grabbed on the run, usually something from the fridge or freezer. It's rare when they sit down to eat with parents and siblings. They enjoy dinner with us as a pleasant novelty, but maybe not as a steady diet. It's a struggle to get our own teenagers to power off their phones during dinner and focus on what's happening right in front of them. Once these kids are out on their own, they'll be just as likely as any of their peers to live on order-in and takeout. I'm not kidding myself.

But once they're full-fledged adults with families of their own? Maybe then they'll begin to eat like normal human beings. Best-case scenario, once they're joined at the table by partners and children they'll learn to cook and adopt more civilized habits. Their notions of what constitutes a healthy diet may also mature, meaning they'll want more control over what they consume. And perhaps they'll recoil at how much money they've been wasting on those exorbitant delivery charges.

For now, however, ordering food via an app-driven delivery service is the young-adult equivalent of yelling, "Mom, I'm hungry; feed me!" If the gratification is not exactly instant, it beats getting up off the sofa, shopping, cooking, and cleaning up.

We can look to one of the culprits, Grubhub, for insights into food trends among the young. The company compiles lists of its users' most popular dishes, and has done so for years. During the spring of 2020, meaning the early months of COVID eating, these were the most common search terms:

1. Wine
2. Cake
3. Boba tea
4. Beer
5. Donuts

(I had to look it up—"boba tea" is another term for "bubble tea," which I also had to look up. It's tea made with tiny balls of tapioca or other starches, often with sugar added, meaning tea that's sweetened for contemporary tastes, with a cute name.)

During that same period, the dishes that had the biggest increases in popularity were:

1. Spicy chicken sandwich
2. Red velvet cupcake
3. Plant-based burger

4. Cajun shrimp chicken pasta
5. Cheeseburger sliders

In other words, three sandwiches, a cupcake, and pasta with shrimp *and* chicken. Don't we all wish we could eat like kids?

According to a recent study, millennials snack four times a day, more than any other age group. It adds up, essentially, to a whole meal—eaten entirely spontaneously, presumably with zero preparation required. This really caught my eye: A marketing survey found that many young people today prefer eating breakfast cereal as snacks, straight out of the box, rather than with milk in a bowl—because the cleanup is too much work. When sticking a bowl and a spoon in the dishwasher becomes an onerous task, we've arrived in uncharted territory.

Having said that, if I were an executive at Kellogg's or General Mills, I'd start packaging all our cereals in small bags, just like candy, pretzels, chips, and popcorn, ready to sell alongside M&M's, Skittles, and Hershey's Kisses. Next to that stuff, even Lucky Charms might seem good for you. It's finally dawning on us that cereal is an unhealthy breakfast, but maybe it will qualify as a healthy-sounding snack.

According to one estimate I've seen, American food companies spend nearly $2 billion a year marketing their products to children, and you can be pretty sure that those videos and other content aren't devoted to the joys of cabbage or sardines. A study by NYU scientists published in the journal *Pediatrics* found that nearly half of the most popular videos from kid influencers promoted food and drinks, and more than 90 percent of those products were unhealthy branded food, drinks, or fast-food toys. Videos featuring junk-food product placements were viewed more than 1 billion times.

As I'm writing this, the United Kingdom just proposed a ban on all junk-food advertising, including whatever appears on social media, even internet search engines. The impact will be monumental once it goes into effect, I believe, which is why the world's biggest manufacturers of food and drink, along with all the media that accept their advertising, lined up against the measure. Their big fear is that it might spread to other countries and influence what we all eat and drink.

Rescuing our kids from the clutches of junk-food hucksters sounds like a worthy goal, and I wish campaigns like this all the luck in the world. But I wonder if big food isn't already too big to tame.

There's something poignant about the efforts to push back. My friend Karen Karp is an activist and entrepreneur who works at creating a healthier and more equitable food environment all over the country. Among her successes has been getting New York City's vast public school system to feed children lunches made with locally grown vegetables and fruits—a great thing for the kids as well as the growers. Farmers even visit classrooms to talk about where their food comes from, which is news to many city kids. Some of those students see for the first time what an eggplant or a tomato looks like! Mind-boggling, I agree, but how could they know, given the current unhealthy state of inner-city food?

Anyway, as you can see—there's hope. Some.

Epilogue

Good thing the end is near—it's almost dinnertime, and I'm ready to pack up and head home.

For the past thirty-five years, I've had the privilege of being able to walk to and from work. It takes about sixteen and a half minutes door-to-door. I'm lucky; I know it—for most workers, the commute is a daily torment that consumes far too many precious waking hours. For me, it's a constant learning experience.

Along the way I pass through what you could call my personal food environment, meaning I walk by a lot of places where things to eat and drink are sold. You have a food environment too. We all do. Yours and mine may differ in some respects, but both are reflections of everything I've been discussing in this book—food, where it comes from, and especially how it is made available to us. There may be no better way of witnessing global change than by paying attention to what we eat and drink. And there's no clearer picture of that than the one we get down here at ground level, in the real—non-digital, non-virtual—world.

The biggest change I'm noticing today is the same one that has transformed most of the planet. It's no surprise by now how much upheaval a pandemic can bring. As I've said already, COVID clobbered the brick-and-mortar world of retail, food included. Hospitality workers—cooks, waiters, and all the others involved—took the biggest hit. We continued to eat, of course, but learned to find pretty much everything we wanted online. That alone brought major disruption to how we relate to our food. Suddenly, grocery buying was missing its tactile, sensual side. Our shopping routine lost some of its adventure and power to educate and surprise. Our nutritional habits suffered, too, as many of us can attest. The more closely connected we are to our food, the healthier we tend to be.

As I write this, it's Vaccine Spring outside. The streets of my commute are once again teeming with pedestrians. True, there are now quite a few vacant storefronts where businesses—grocers, restaurants, and bars among them—once flourished. Maybe they were quietly vulnerable even before COVID came along to shut them down for good. But many of the establishments along my walk have weathered the storm and are back, nearly as lively as before. It's going to take some time before we understand the real and lasting impact of the pandemic. If workers don't return to their offices and shops, they won't be having lunch or drinks or snacks or dinner in this neighborhood. So we may be in the early stages of a slow-motion transformation with no end in sight.

Even pre-COVID, I'd been watching how dramatically my food environment has been changing in recent years. For one thing, there are now a lot more places to acquire things to eat and drink. More ethnic restaurants, cookie shops, health-food boutiques, luncheonettes, fast-food outlets, vegan cafés, supermarkets, open-air stands, coffee shops, food trucks . . . I can go into an office supply store and buy a barrel of candy or pretzels, or I can visit a discount shoe store and buy caramel-coated popcorn or a protein bar. There's a high-end health club I pass with what looks like a fancy café right inside the big front windows, which means somebody thinks this will help attract new members. There's a bookstore with a decent coffee shop that also serves wine and sandwiches. A whole lot of feeding going on.

This is where all our best and worst nutritional impulses exist side by side, the highs and lows of how we eat right now. A couple times a week, I'll stop at the lively farmers market that's on my way home. I can stand in the middle of the homespun growers and artisans and look to the right and see a big Whole Foods store that's usually packed, and to the left and view a McDonald's that's also always crowded.

Here's a combination juice bar/smoothie shop/ice-cream parlor, and sitting outside is a young guy about to dig into something I will try to describe: it looks like a giant sundae, and rising out of the cup are what appear to be pink and white cotton candy clouds, suspended on very thin wires. He catches me staring and announces, "It's my birthday!"

To the right up ahead is an Indian restaurant I love. The food is excellent, the décor is elegant, and the prices are high—but worth every rupee. When I first moved to this city, there was (and still is) a whole neighborhood of Indian restaurants downtown. The décor down there is bare-bones, the prices are rock-bottom, and the food is basic but terrific—a magnet for adventurous young eaters. Before you go in, you stop at the deli on the corner and buy a big bottle of Kingfisher beer, brewed in Bangalore.

This has been the trajectory of ethnic eating in America. The restaurants start out superauthentic and modestly priced, perfect for fellow immigrants who usually don't have a lot of cash to blow on dining out, but also welcoming to the rest of us willing to try. Then, as upward mobility does its job, the restaurants become more sophisticated, and the prices rise to match the loftier ambitions. In this city you can still find all kinds of ethnic food at student-friendly prices, but those same cuisines now also occupy the upper reaches of the big-city dining-out experience—deservedly. I read online a complaint about a Mexican restaurant where dinner for two was nearly $200. The guy was shocked. Maybe he's had too much Taco Bell. But what did he think rich Mexicans eat when they go out to dinner—burritos?

We're now approaching what's still known as "the *Sex and the City* block"—the street where exteriors for the legendary TV series, which began in 1998, were shot. For the first few seasons, a very picturesque town house here was depicted as the home of the show's main character. The people who actually lived in that building had to ask tour buses to please no longer stop out front, and they even got Google Maps to blur the image of their home. Still, many years later, fans of the series and the movie spin-offs continue to come and worship at the site.

Coincidentally, the star of the show, Sarah Jessica Parker, and her family live right around the corner, and as far as I know, they're not among the stops on the tour. But visitors continue to flock to the Magnolia Bakery, which was also featured in the series. There are often lines outside of people waiting to buy cupcakes and, for some weird reason, banana pudding. Some take their goodies to the park across the street and eat there, and fill the trash cans until they overflow, adding to the typical city vexations of rodents and insects. I've actually walked into the store and asked the manager if he'd come to my doorstep and clean up the debris left by his customers. As of this writing, I'm still waiting. . . .

Once, we were all content to buy our various nut butters in jars, as the big brands produced them. Then, the rebellious, health-conscious, all-natural entrepreneurs started making inroads. Today, I love being able to come to the fancy little health-food shop across the street and grind my own almond butter, even though it costs more than having somebody grind it for me. Where's the logic there? My almond butter is 100 percent almonds, which I pour into the grinder and watch as they emerge from the other end—no added salt, sugar, or oil, no unknown industrial processes involved, no mysteries. Just me and my nuts. Someday, will we all rise up against the Skippys and Jifs of the world?

Here's the Korean restaurant where I've eaten a lot, particularly after a long day at the office. Bulgogi with *gochujang* is my standard order. To me, it's not so exotic—it was something I ate often during the early seventies, when I was a student at a Korean university. Ramen and bulgogi were our staples. Bulgogi is just roast meat—occasionally, tofu—served over fresh and pickled vegetables and rice. Couldn't be simpler, except for the *gochujang*, the spicy, sweet sauce Koreans use on everything. I love it—it's sort of like a spice bomb hit a candy factory.

I'm fascinated by ethnic crossovers, like the Korean taco, where you take that bulgogi and stick it into the context of a taco. And it goes from something you eat with chopsticks to food you can hold in one hand and devour as you walk down the street. Even if you're not a fan of ambulatory eating (as I am *not*), you have to admit it's a significant shift in how we interact with our food. For all the ethnic strife and immigration anxiety we're experiencing right now, it's encouraging to watch Korea and Mexico find common ground in American foodways. There's a hopeful metaphor in there somewhere.

Multicultural tacos are the particular province of food trucks, and we're walking by quite a few of those. You can go to midtown Manhattan or any other urban setting and find some pretty elaborate trucks with long lines of office workers waiting to buy lunch. The trucks have become so entrenched, such a part of the city food landscape, that if you go onto Yelp, you'll find reviews for food trucks right alongside those of brick-and-mortar restaurants. The food truck has become the frontier of mobile haute cuisine. When I first worked in midtown Manhattan, my street food of choice was a hot dog and a Coke.

Here's an outpost of an ultra-fancy *gelateria* and *cioccolateria*—meaning an Italian store that sells ice cream and candy. Absolutely the most beautiful, elegant place I'll see on my way home, possibly one of the most gorgeous shops in the city. A small cone of gelato here sells for $5. There are plenty of customers. A few steps down the street, on the corner, is a Mister Softee truck, where a cone of soft serve goes for $3. There's a line there too. And we have no reason to think that Mister Softee's customer today won't be eating expensive Italian *gianduja* (chocolate-hazelnut) gelato tomorrow, and vice versa. It's that high-low food dynamic at work.

A little farther along and we're at one of my favorite stops, Murray's Cheese. Until recently it was owned by my friend Rob, who came from a grocery family in New Jersey. He was in the city one day and wandered by a cheese shop with a sign in the window that said: "We're Closing." He looked inside and thought, *Maybe I should make an offer?* The owner was willing to sell for a tiny amount of money. Rob, being the enterprising guy that he is, rented a better space across the street, moved the counters over, and for the next ten years stood there, curating (and cutting) cheese. Just like that he went from intrigued bystander to entrepreneurial artisan. A lot of stories in the world of food start that way.

I've been to many cheese stores, in France and elsewhere, and I remember a really amazing one in Lausanne, Switzerland. But Murray's is something special. Each cheese they sell has a label telling you precisely where it's from and what exactly it's made from—its life story, practically. Today, we all desire food narratives; we want to know the things we eat and drink in a way we never could (or cared to) before.

Murray's even runs a school, a place where you can pay for the privilege of learning how to eat cheese. And plenty of people do, which maybe isn't so crazy considering how much money you can spend on the stuff. The funny part is you could probably go to the grocer down the street and buy the same cheeses for less money—but without the stories.

Today, in the food world, those narratives have a value of their own. We want to know practically everything about what we're eating before we eat it. One of the funniest sketches on the comedy series *Portlandia* featured a couple in a restaurant about to order the chicken, but first they wanted to see the farm where the bird was raised, to make certain it had enjoyed a happy, healthy, life-affirming existence before it ended up on their plates. (Sure thing, the waitress said, and even agreed to hold their table until they got back.)

Here's a famous coffee store, a neighborhood institution, that mainly sells beans, of every kind imaginable, and has been selling them for several decades. You can also buy a cup of coffee here, which makes the experience something more than mere food shopping—partly because it means you can sample before you buy, and socialize a little too. I remember having a conversation with Howard Schultz in Seattle in 1988, back when he had forty shops and was still trying to figure out whether Starbucks was going to be a bean store that sells beverages or a beverage store that sells beans. He discovered the same answer that this venerable old shop had found many years before: you can be both.

Way back in 1994, Bill Gates said something prophetic: "Banking is necessary. Banks are not." Most of us didn't get the full implications of that statement then, but we sure do now. In many instances, the digital age has made brick-and-mortar existence redundant, if not downright obsolete, especially in our shopping lives. Entire categories of retail stores, once ubiquitous, have been wiped out. Gone. Never to return. The hegemony of physical place had already been fading.

COVID took that trend and filled it with rocket fuel. The internet has made every place equal to every other. At least on the internet.

We shop today not from stores but from platforms.

As a result, the world of shopping has become a buyers' market. Prices won't be determined by manufacturers *or* retailers—they'll be dynamic and set by what we consumers are willing to pay. Everything— cost, volume discounts, shipping fees, taxes—will vary depending on who's selling and who's buying. We won't know whom we're buying from, or where (if anywhere) they're located. It won't matter. You and I now hold every store in the world in our hand. Let's hope we know what we're doing.

And yet food, for all the transformation it has undergone, has managed to resist a total e-commerce takeover. I suspect it always will. We still possess an ancient desire to see, to smell, to touch most of the things we'll eat and drink. I don't think even Bill Gates would disagree.

I'm nearly at the end of my walk now, which is where I usually find Harry. That's not his real name—he's an immigrant; it's easy to tell by his accent. But it's his American handle, for the benefit of people like me. Harry runs a produce stand on the corner of my block. It's basically a long folding table piled high with a remarkable variety of vegetables and fruits. He stands there behind it, morning to night, day after day. In cities all over the world there are small businesses like this one, run by entrepreneurs like Harry. He puts a lot of effort into this stand—everything is arranged just so, with carefully hand-lettered price signs, and it makes a beautiful sight. It all looks so fresh and clean and healthy, it's hard for me *not* to shop here.

When I discovered Harry was from Turkey, I tried out a little of the Turkish I've picked up from my wife, and he laughed. When I see him, I say, "Meraba?"—how are you?—and he grins and says, "Meraba" back. But Harry doesn't know anything about me, or what I do for a living. When I offer advice about his signs, he smiles and nods—to him I'm just another customer, a slightly eccentric one who thinks he knows something about how to sell produce.

Harry and I have a regular routine by now: I'll ask for cucumbers, say, or avocados, and he'll ask when I'm going to eat them. If it's tonight, he'll choose some that are ripe and ready. If I say they're going into the fridge, to be eaten later, I'll get something nearly ripe but not quite—so it will be perfect when I serve it. Let's see online grocery shopping do that.

"Harry," I say tonight, "I need a few tomatoes."

"When will you eat them?" he asks.

"Maybe tomorrow," I say.

He narrows his eyes and examines his stock.

"Here," Harry says, picking three. *"These."*

Acknowledgments

What a tough ride. In March 2020, as COVID-19 hit, a third of this manuscript had to be tossed. The rules and perspective on a post-pandemic world and the purpose of this volume rethought. Coming out of a miserable year, we needed a positive spin on where we are going and how we are going to get there. We are what we eat. If we can get greener, more local and healthier, we have to be more aware. I hope you have liked and responded to what you have read. I have so many people to thank for their support and encouragement.

Pieces of this book's content came from columns written over the years for design:retail and The Robin Report (TRR). Alison Medina, Doug Hope, Jessie Dowd, Michelle Havich, Toni Ward at Emerald Expo, publishers of design:retail have been in my corner for more than fifteen years. My good friends Robin Lewis and Deborah Patton at TRR have poked and edited my material for years. In their lineup of distinguished and accomplished columnists, I've felt often like a big copper penny in a pile of gold doubloons. Deborah is the best editor I've ever worked for. We have known each other in a past life.

Over two years of work on the manuscript, I've had countless conversations, some recorded and transcribed, others just as intense and real but over phones, meals, and adult beverages. A few of those names and conversations made it into this document—Kevin Kelley, Victor Verlage, Ramon Portilla, Rob Easley, Marion Nestle, Kristal Arabian, Ken Park, and Nina Planck—but many others helped set the stage.

Over the past thirty-five years of interaction with the retail, tech, architecture, and design community, I've had friendships that vacillated from professional to personal: Denny Gerteman, Aaron Spiess, Judy Bell, Chuck Luckenbill, Chuck Palmer, Kristoffer Reiter, Richard Kelly, Michael Gould, Rob LoCasio, Kate Newlin, Andrea Dorigo, Wendy Liebmann, Jalal Hamad, Ken Pray, Nancy Bass Wyden, Tony Spring, Taylor Kristov, Samantha Klein, Matt Winn, Alan O'Neill, James Damain, and the lovely Leiti Hsu.

One of the most difficult results of COVID-19 has been my grounding. This is the longest period in my life I've not been on an airplane. Over the past thirty-five years I've spent more than 120 nights a year on the road. The company I founded worked in forty-seven countries, and I personally have lectured and or consulted in even more places. From Japan and China, to Australia, Africa, Russia, South America, and Europe—I have friends and colleagues I've missed whom historically I've seen regularly. My father the diplomat described his global friendships as "pump and suck"—people he saw intermittently, but those meetings were about the exchange of high volumes of information. The levels of trust and confidence are not about the amount of time spent together but about the intensity.

I have a posse too. Friends I've made over the years who contributed to who I am and what I do, and yet their most important role has been keeping us collectively grounded. Christine Lehner and Rip Hayman, I've known for more than fifty years. Roberto Brambilla and Carmen Spofford mentored me at an early age and continue to listen, point, and laugh. Patrick Rodmell, Rob Kaufelt, Ramon Portilla, Kaz Toyota, Pierre Cournot, Barry Burgess, Holland Williams, John Barkley, Joseph Guglietti, Bruce Carpenter—all my aging brothers. Thanks.

Any author has a community of fellow writers who form his network. Robert Spector, another retail-focused writer; David Bosshart, director of Swiss thinktank GDI; Martin Lindstrom the global visionary; Allen Adamson the branding expert; Craig Unger the author of political books; Michael Gross, a historian of social New York City; Andy Cohen, a magician and motivational author; and Faith Popcorn, the business reinventor, are just a few.

I have a group of young coworkers who have shared my passion to our part of the market research world—Liam O'Connell, Adam Kavett, Larissa Hunt, and Patty Maltez. I wish them well in carrying the ball forward.

Glen Hartley has been my agent for more than twenty years. Like many others, I have mourned the passing of Alice Mayhew, the editor of three of my books at Simon & Schuster, in the winter of 2020. No other person has more single-handedly been responsible for the rewriting of American history. Stephanie Frerich has stepped into the role as my editor. She has been a joy to work with. Jonathan Karp—I remain a proud S&S author.

Finally, thanks to Bill Tonelli for your patience, point of view, and hard work.

Index

About the Author

PACO UNDERHILL is the founder of Envirosell, Inc., a global research and consulting firm. His clients include more than a third of the Fortune 100 list, and he has worked on supermarkets, convenience store, food, beverage, and restaurant issues in fifty countries. He has written articles for or been profiled in the *New York Times*, the *Wall Street Journal*, the *Washington Post*, the *New Yorker*, *Smithsonian Magazine*, and more. Paco divides his time between his homes in New York City and Madison, Connecticut.